MASTER THE BASICS:

FRENCH

by
Christopher Kendris

B.S., M.S., Columbia University in the City of New York
M.A., Ph.D., Northwestern University in Evanston, Illinois

Diplômé, Faculté des Lettres, Université de Paris
et Institut de Phonétique, Paris (en Sorbonne)

Formerly Assistant Professor
Department of French and Spanish
State University of New York
Albany, New York

BARRON'S

Barron's Educational Series, Inc.

To the sweet memory of my mother
and to the memory of my father

All inquiries should be addressed to:
Barron's Educational Series, Inc.
250 Wireless Boulevard
Hauppauge, New York 11788

Library of Congress Catalog Card No. 87-1407
International Standard Book No. 0-8120-3762-6

Library of Congress Cataloging-in-Publication Data

Kendris, Christopher.
    Master the basics: French.

    Includes index.
    1. French language—Text-books for foreign speakers—
English. 2. French language—Grammar—1950—
I. Title.
PC2129.E5K44   1987   448.2'421   87-1407
ISBN 0-8120-3762-6

PRINTED IN THE UNITED STATES OF AMERICA

456   9792   987

For St. Sophia Greek Orthodox Church of Albany, New York,
my parish
and
For my three grandsons
Bryan, Daniel, Matthew
with love

Contents

Preface

This book is one of a new miniseries of language grammar reviews. It is designed to help you brush up on your French grammar for instant communication and comprehension. The numerical arrangement gives you fast and easy access to what you need to know or verify.

Beginning on p. 3 there is a diagnostic test that you ought to take immediately. It consists of sixty questions. Three questions are taken from each of the twenty chapters listed in the table of contents as sections §1. through §20. Take the test to find out what you know, what you don't know, and where your strengths and weaknesses lie. Answers are explained at the end of the diagnostic test. There you will also find an analysis of the question numbers and the § numbers. In this way, you can refer to a particular § number where your answers were not correct and brush up where needed. The complete brush-up section consists of three parts: the Basics, the Parts of Speech, and Special Topics, all of which are outlined in the table of contents.

Occasionally I offer some mnemonic (memory) tips to help you remember certain aspects of French grammar and vocabulary. For example, if you cannot remember whether the French word for twenty (**vingt**) is spelled *ng* or *gn*, remember it this way:

Mnemonic tip	*V I*	*N*	*G T*
	T W E	N	T Y

Mnemonic devices are very useful in learning and remembering. Students learn and remember in different ways. What works for you may not work for someone else. You must think of ways to help yourself remember. If you think of a way that seems foolish, don't tell anyone; just let it work for you. One of my students in a Spanish class, for example, told me that she finally figured out a way to remember the meaning of the Spanish verb *buscar* / to look for. She said, "I'm looking for a bus or a car." How many mnemonic tips can you make up in French? Here are a few more: If someone asks you, "What are the five major

Romance Languages?'' are you going to say you don't know? Remember **FRIPS:**

Mnemonic tip

French
Romanian
Italian
Portuguese
Spanish

To remember that there are only four nasal vowels in French, hang on to this catchy phrase because each word contains one of the four nasal vowels:

Mnemonic tip

un bon vin blanc / **a good white wine**

If you keep pronouncing *un œuf* / an egg incorrectly, say this out loud:

Mnemonic tip

Do you want one egg? Two eggs?
One egg is enough!
One egg is *un œuf*!

The sound of the English word ''enough'' is very close to the sound of the French word *un œuf.*

There are many more mnemonic tips throughout this book. If I have omitted anything you think is important, if you spot any misprints, or if you have any suggestions for the improvement of the next edition, please write to me, care of the publisher.

Christopher Kendris
B.S., M.S., M.A., Ph.D.

How to Use This Book

To get the most out of *Master the Basics: French,* follow these steps:

Step 1 The first thing you should do is to become familiar with this book. Turn the pages and look at each page for a few seconds. When you reach the table of contents, examine it carefully. If you find something that strikes your interest, turn to that section to see exactly what is there. Do you want to know when the subjunctive should be used? Fan the pages until you come to §7.15 or go straight to the page given in the contents. I'm sure you will find §11. of special interest and value. Do not begin any studying until you have reviewed every page. It won't take more than about ten minutes.

Step 2 Now take the diagnostic test, which begins on p. 3. At the end of that preliminary test, you will find the Explained Answers and a Diagnostic Analysis. Check the question numbers that you had right or wrong and, if wrong, turn to the appropriate section and study it, making certain you understand the explanations so that you can learn more about that particular element of French. If you happen to have many answers right, do not assume that you know that particular element of French thoroughly. Asking only three questions from each of the twenty sections is just to give you an idea of your strengths and weaknesses.

Step 3 The next step is to go through the entire Grammar Brush-Up, reviewing some portions and studying others in depth. The final part of this book is Let's Review. You can do the more than two hundred exercises and activities in this section either after having done the Grammar Brush-Up or as you work through the book. The questions are keyed to the numerical reference system in the Brush-Up and Answers sections. Another possibility is to do both: Try the questions corresponding to each chapter after you have studied the chapter, and then do them again for a final review after you have worked through the entire Brush-Up.

The French-English vocabulary will be useful as you practice your French, and the index provides an easy reference to any basic grammatical point that you may want to check.

Now begin with Step 1!

FIND OUT WHAT YOU KNOW

This diagnostic test covers material presented in the Basics, the Parts of Speech, and Special Topics, all of which are included in §1.—§20. in this book. On page xi, where you find the section on how to use this book, read Step 2 again. That's what this diagnostic test is all about.

Test Yourself

Choose the correct answer by circling the letter. Do not refer to the Answer Key and Explained Answers until after you have answered all 60 questions. Time limit is 60 minutes.

THE BASICS

1. In French the vowel combination *eu* in *leur* is pronounced something like the *u* in the English word
   A. up   B. cute   C. urgent   D. you

2. In French the word *bonne* is pronounced like the English word
   A. bun   B. bone   C. bean   D. ban

3. In French the word *père*, containing the accent grave on *è*, is pronounced very much like the English word
   A. peer   B. pear   C. pour   D. pure

4. The French word for semicolon is
   A. *point*   B. *deux points*   C. *virgule*
   D. *point virgule*

5. The number of syllables in the French word *comprendre* is
   A. 2   B. 3   C. 4   D. 5

6. The four nasal vowels in French are found in the following catchy phrase
   A. *un bon vin rouge*   B. *un bon crayon blanc*
   C. *un bon fromage français*   D. *un bon vin blanc*

PARTS OF SPEECH

7. There are ____ definite articles in French and they all mean "the."
   A. two   B. three   C. four   D. five

8. When the preposition *à* is in front of the definite article *le*, it contracts to
   A. *au*   B. *aux*   C. *du*   D. *des*

9. When the preposition *de* is in front of the definite article *le*, it contracts to
   A. *au*   B. *aux*   C. *du*   D. *des*

10. A typical example of a feminine singular French noun is
    A. *logement*   B. *fromage*   C. *chapeau*
    D. *attention*

3

11. A typical example of a masculine singular French noun is
 A. *fourchette*   B. *chance*   C. *gâteau*
 D. *sucette*

12. A typical example of a French noun that is spelled the same in the singular and plural is
 A. *bras*   B. *livre*   C. *journal*   D. *feu*

13. The demonstrative adjective that precedes a masculine singular noun beginning with a vowel or silent *h* is
 A. *ce*   B. *cet*   C. *cette*   D. *ces*

14. The demonstrative adjective that precedes a feminine singular noun, whether it begins with a consonant, a vowel, or a silent *h* is
 A. *ce*   B. *cet*   C. *cette*   D. *ces*

15. The possessive adjective in front of a feminine singular noun beginning with a vowel or silent *h* (for example, *amie*) is
 A. *ma*   B. *mon*   C. *mes*   D. *m'*

Of the four choices given, select the response to each question that is sensible and grammatically correct.

16. *Avez-vous des frères?*
 A. *Oui, vous avez des frères.*   B. *Oui, j'ai frères.*
 C. *Oui, j'en ai.*   D. *Oui, il a des frères.*

17. *Est-ce que les fleurs sont sur la table?*
 A. *Oui, ils sont sur la table.*   B. *Oui, ils y sont.*
 C. *Oui, elles y sont.*   D. *Oui, la table est sur les fleurs.*

18. *Est-ce que vous lisez la lettre?*
 A. *Oui, vous lisez la lettre.*   B. *Oui, vous la lisez.*
 C. *Oui, je le lis.*   D. *Oui, je la lis.*

On the blank line write the correct form of the past participle of the verb given in parentheses.

19. *(aller)*   *Mon amie Jacqueline est* _____ *au cinéma avec Robert.*

20. *(laver)*   *Marguerite s'est* _____ *avant de manger.*

21. *(partir)*   *Mes sœurs sont* _____ *pour la France hier.*

Write one adverb in French ending in -*ment* that is formed from a feminine singular adjective.

22. _____

Answer the following question in French in the affirmative; in other words, write in French, "Yes, I do like French."

23. *N'aimez-vous pas le français?* _____

Translate the following sentence into French.

24. Henry works better than Robert. _____

_____

Fill in the blank with *vers* or *envers,* whichever is appropriate.

25. *Pourquoi allez-vous* _____ *la porte?*

26. *J'ai beaucoup de respect* _____ *les vieilles personnes.*

Translate the following sentence into French.

27. Robert did that within an hour. _____

Write the French for each of the following conjunctions.

28. therefore _____ 29. unless _____ 30. whereas _____

SPECIAL TOPICS

The following sentences are scrambled. Unscramble the words and write them in the correct order.

31. *donne / me / pas / ne / les / il.* _____

32. *ne / ai / lui / le / je / donné / pas.* _____

33. *ne / pas / Yvonne / s'est / lavée.* _____

Of the four choices given, select the correct verb form and write it in the blank.

34. *J'___ l'autobus depuis vingt minutes quand il est arrivé.*
    A. *attends*   B. *ai attendu*   C. *attendrais*
    D. *attendais*

35. *Il y a vingt minutes que j'* _____ *l'autobus.*
    A. *attend*   B. *attends*   C. *ai attendu*
    D. *attendrais*

36. *Madame Martin est partie il y* _____ *une heure.*
    A. *avait*   B. *a*   C. *aurait*   D. *a eu*

Each of the following sentences is incomplete. Of the four choices given, select the one that makes a grammatically correct sentence and circle the letter of your choice.

37. *Quelle est la date aujourd'hui? C'est* _____ *octobre.*
    A. *l'un*   B. *le premier d'*   C. *l'un d'*
    D. *le premier*

38. *Je vais en France* _____ *juillet.*
    A. *au*   B. *dans*   C. *en*   D. *à*

39. *En* _____ *il neige souvent à Paris.*
    A. *été*   B. *printemps*   C. *automne*   D. *hiver*

Study the clocks and underneath each one write in French the time that is given.

40.
_____

41.
_____

42.
_____

Study these three drawings and underneath each one write in French a statement about the weather.

43.
_____

44.
_____

45.
_____

Write the required number in French for the following.

46. *Comptez par dix. Dix, vingt, trente,* _____

47. *Sept fois huit font* _____

48. What number in French sounds like the English word "says"? _____

Write a French synonym for what is given.

49. *aimer mieux* _____

50. *une erreur* _____

51. *brève* _____

Write an antonym in French for what is given.

52. *absente* _____

53. *la beauté* _____

54. *perdre* _____

Write the French word and the definite article for each of the following cognates.

55. photography _____

56. memory _____

57. dictionary _____

Write the English meaning for each of the following false cognates.

58. *les actualités* _____

59. large _____

60. *le raisin* _____

Explained Answers

RIGHT   WRONG
   (check one)

_____   _____   1. C   *see* §1.

_____   _____   2. A   *see* §1.

_____   _____   3. B   *see* §1.

_____   _____   4. D   *see* §2.

_____   _____   5. B   *see* §2.

_____   _____   6. D   *see* §2.

_____   _____   7. C   *see* §3.1.

_____   _____   8. A   *see* §3.1.

_____   _____   9. C   *see* §3.1.

_____   _____   10. D   *see* §4.1 and §4.2.

_____   _____   11. C   *see* §4.1 and §4.2.

_____   _____   12. A   *see* §4.1 and §4.2.

_____   _____   13. B   *see* §5.4 – 2.

_____   _____   14. C   *see* §5.4 – 2.

_____   _____   15. B   *see* §5.4 – 4.

_____   _____   16. C   *see* §6.1 – 5.

_____   _____   17. C   *see* §6.1 – 6.

_____   _____   18. D   The direct object *la lettre* is replaced by the feminine direct object pronoun, *la.*   *see* §6.1 – 2.

_____   _____   19. *allée.* You need to add *e* to the past participle *allé* to make it feminine because the verb is conjugated with *être (est)* and the subject is feminine.   *see* §7.1.

_____   _____   20. *lavée.* You need to add *e* to the past participle *lavé* to make it feminine because the reflexive pronoun *s'* is feminine and serves as the preceding direct object pronoun; it refers to the subject, *Marguerite,* which is feminine.   *see* §7.1.

_____   _____   21. *parties.* You need to add *e* to the past participle *parti* to make it feminine because the verb is conjugated with *être (sont)* and the subject, *mes sœurs,* is feminine. It is also plural, so you must also add *s* to the past participle.   *see* §7.1 and §7.3 – 1.

8

RIGHT   WRONG
(check one)

22. *seulement.* Several examples are given in **§8.1.** Review it.

23. *Si, j'aime le français.*   see **§8.4.**

24. *Henri travaille mieux que Robert.*   see **§8.3 – 3.**

25. *vers*   see **§9.**

26. *envers*   see **§9.**

27. *Robert a fait cela en une heure.*   see **§9.**

28. *donc*   see **§10.**

29. *à moins que*   see **§10.**

30. *tandis que*   see **§10.**

31. *Il ne me les donne pas.*   see **§11.**

32. *Je ne le lui ai pas donné.*   see **§11.**

33. *Yvonne ne s'est pas lavée.*   see **§11.**

34. D   You need the imperfect indicative because the verb in the other clause is in the *passé composé.*   see **§12.**

35. A   You need the present tense because the verb in the other clause is in the present tense (the *a* in the expression *il y a*).   see **§12.1.**

36. B   You need the present tense of *avoir* because *il y a* + a length of time means *ago.*   see **§12.1.**

37. D   see **§13.**

38. C   see **§13.**

39. D   see **§13.**

40. *Il est cinq heures dix.*   see **§14.**

41. *Il est une heure.*   see **§14.**

42. *Il est six heures moins le quart.*   see **§14.**

43. *Il pleut.*   see **§15.**

44. *Il neige.*   see **§15.**

45. *Il fait du soleil.* OR *Il fait soleil.*   see **§15.**

46. *quarante*   see **§16.**

47. *cinquante-six*   see **§16.**

48. *seize*   see **§16.**

RIGHT   WRONG
(check one)

_____   _____   49. *préférer* *see* **§17.**

_____   _____   50. *une faute* *see* **§17.**

_____   _____   51. *courte* You are given *brève* in the feminine singular form; therefore, you must write *courte,* which is also feminine singular. *see* **§17.**

_____   _____   52. *présente* You are given *absente* in the feminine singular form; therefore, you must write *présente,* which is feminine singular. *see* **§18.**

_____   _____   53. *la laideur* *see* **§18.**

_____   _____   54. *trouver* *see* **§18.**

_____   _____   55. *la photographie* *see* **§19.**

_____   _____   56. *la mémoire* *see* **§19.**

_____   _____   57. *le dictionnaire* *see* **§19.**

_____   _____   58. news reports *see* **§20.**

_____   _____   59. wide *see* **§20.**

_____   _____   60. grape *see* **§20.**

Diagnostic Analysis

Section	Question Numbers	Number of Answers	
		Right	Wrong
THE BASICS			
1. Pronunciation	1, 2, 3		
2. Capitalization, Punctuation, Word Division	4, 5, 6		
THE PARTS OF SPEECH			
3. Articles	7, 8, 9		
4. Nouns	10, 11, 12		
5. Adjectives	13, 14, 15		
6. Pronouns	16, 17, 18		
7. Verbs	19, 20, 21		
8. Adverbs	22, 23, 24		
9. Prepositions	25, 26, 27		
10. Conjunctions	28, 29, 30		
SPECIAL TOPICS			
11. Word Order	31, 32, 33		
12. Idioms	34, 35, 36		
13. Dates, Days, Months, Seasons	37, 38, 39		
14. Telling Time	40, 41, 42		
15. Talking About the Weather	43, 44, 45		
16. Numbers	46, 47, 48		
17. Synonyms	49, 50, 51		
18. Antonyms	52, 53, 54		
19. Cognates	55, 56, 57		
20. Tricky Words	58, 59, 60		
TOTAL QUESTIONS:	60		

Use the following scale to see how you did.

58 to 60 right:	Excellent
55 to 57 right:	Very Good
52 to 54 right:	Average
49 to 51 right:	Below Average
Fewer than 49 right:	Unsatisfactory

A GRAMMAR BRUSH-UP

In the chapters that follow, a numerical decimal system has been used with the symbol § in front of it. This was done so that you may find quickly and easily the reference to a particular point in basic French grammar when you use the index. For example, if you look up the entry ''adjectives'' in the index, you will find the reference given as §5. Sometimes additional § reference numbers are given when the entry you consult is mentioned in other areas in the chapter §. The index also includes some key French words, for example, avoir and être, with § references also given to them.

The Basics

§1.

Guide to Pronouncing French Sounds

English words given here contain sounds that only approximate French sounds.

PURE VOWEL SOUNDS

Pronounced as in the

French word	English word
la	at
pas	ah!
été	ate
ère	egg
ici	see
hôtel	over
donne	bun
ou	too
leur	urgent
deux	pudding
tu	cute
le	ago

NASAL VOWEL SOUNDS

un	unguent
bon	song
vin	sang
blanc	dong

SEMICONSONANT SOUNDS

oui	west
huit	you eat
fille	yes, see ya later

CONSONANT SOUNDS

bonne	bun
dans	dong
fou	first, pharmacy
garçon	go
je	measure
chose	shake
café, qui	cap, kennel
le	let
mette	met
nette	net

CONSONANT SOUNDS
Pronounced as in the

French word	English word
montagne)	canyon, onion, union
père	pear
rose	rose
si	see
te	lot
vous	vine
zèbre	zebra
ça	sorry

- If you can, give equal stress to all syllables in a French word; in other words, do not raise your voice on any particular syllable.
- If you can't give equal stress to all syllables in a French word, then raise your voice slightly on the last syllable.

  EXAMPLES:
  chapeau (shah-PO), *magazine* (mah-gah-ZEEN), *perspicacité* (per-spee-kah-see-TAY)

- Do not pronounce the last letter of a French word if it is a consonant.

  EXAMPLES:
  beaucoup (bo-KOO), *aéroport* (ah-air-o-POR)

Some common exceptions: *parc* (pARK), *chef* (shEFF), *avec* (ah-VEK). If you're not sure, don't pronounce the last consonant at all.

| Mnemonic tip | If you don't know which is *accent aigu* (acute) *(é)* and which is *accent grave (è)*, remember that the patient died of acute appendicitis *(é)* and ended up in the grave *(è)*. |

§2.

Capitalization, Punctuation Marks, and Word Division

§2.1 CAPITALIZA- TION

Generally speaking, do not capitalize days of the week, months of the year, languages, nationalities, and religions.

dimanche, lundi, mardi, etc.; janvier, février, mars, etc.; français, espagnol, anglais, etc.; Antonio est italien, María est espagnole; Pierre est français; Jacques est catholique.

§2.2 PUNCTUATION MARKS

The basic punctuation marks in French are:

le point / period   .
point virgule / semicolon   ;
la virgule / comma   ,
l'apostrophe (f) / apostrophe   '
deux points / colon   :
les parenthèses (f) / parentheses   ( )
les guillemets (m) / quotation marks   « »
le point d'interrogation / question mark   ?
les points de suspension / ellipses points   . . .

It is good to know how to divide a word into syllables (not only in French but also in English) because it helps you pronounce and spell the word correctly.

§2.3 WORD DIVISION

Basic Rules

- A syllable must contain a vowel, but it may contain only one vowel and no consonant.

  é / *cole* (*école* / school)

- When you are dealing with single separate consonants, each consonant remains with the vowel that follows it.

  beau / *coup* (*beaucoup* / many, much)

- When two consonants come together, they are separated; the first remains with the preceding syllable and the second remains with the following syllable.

  im / *por* / *tant* (*important*)

17

But if the second of the two consonants that come together is *l* or *r,* do not separate them:

a | près (*après* | after); *im | meu | ble* (*immeuble* | apartment building)

• When three consonants come together, the first two remain with the preceding vowel and the third remains with the vowel that follows it.

ins | ti | tut (*institut*)

But if the third of the three consonants is *l* or *r,* do not separate that third consonant from the second; it remains with the second consonant.

com | pren | dre (*comprendre* | to understand)

Vowels

• Two vowels together are generally separated if they are strong vowels *(a, e, o).*

a | é | ro | port (*aéroport* | airport)

But if you are dealing with a weak vowel *(i, u),* it ordinarily remains in the same syllable with its neighboring vowel, especially if that other vowel is a strong vowel.

huî | tre (*huître* | oyster)

Nasal Vowels

• There are only four nasal vowels in French. You can remember them with the following catchy phrase:

un bon vin blanc | a good white wine

The Parts of Speech

Articles

**§3.1
DEFINITE
ARTICLE**

The definite article in French has four forms, and they all mean "the":

Gender	Singular	Plural
Masculine	*le, l'*	*les*
Feminine	*la, l'*	*les*

Singular	Plural
le garçon / the boy *l'arbre* (m) / the tree *la jeune fille* / the girl *l'actrice* / the actress	*les garçons* / the boys *les arbres* / the trees *les jeunes filles* / the girls *les actrices* / the actresses

**Definite Article
Used**

WITH NOUNS

- Before each noun even when more than one noun is stated.

   J'ai le livre et le cahier. / I have the book and notebook.

- When you make a general statement.

   J'aime le lait. / I like milk.
   J'aime l'été. / I like summer.

- With a noun of weight or measure to express "a," "an," "per."

   dix francs la livre / ten francs a pound
   vingt francs la douzaine / twenty francs a dozen

- Before a noun indicating a profession, rank, or title followed by the name of the person.

   Le professeur Poulin est absent aujourd'hui. / Professor Poulin is absent today.

19

- With the name of a language.

  J'étudie le français. / I'm studying French.

  EXCEPTION: Do *not* use the definite article when the name of a language directly follows a form of the verb *parler.*

  Je parle français et russe. / I speak French and·Russian.

- With the days of the week to indicate an action that is habitually repeated.

  Le samedi je vais au cinéma. / On Saturdays I go to the movies.

  But when you want to indicate a *particular* day, do not use the definite article.

  Samedi je vais au cinéma. / Saturday I am going to the movies. (understood: this Saturday)

- With parts of the body or articles of clothing if the possessor is clearly stated.

  Luigi, qui est italien, a les cheveux noirs. / Luigi, who is Italian, has black hair.

- With family names in the plural, in which case the spelling of the family name does not change.

  Nous allons chez les Durand. / We're going to the Durands.

WITH PREPOSITIONS
- When the prepositions *à* and *de* come before the definite article, it contracts as follows:

Preposition		Article		Contraction
à {	+	le	>	*au*
	+	les	>	*aux*
de {	+	le	>	*du*
	+	les	>	*des*

But there is *no* change with *l'* or *la.*

Je vais à l'aéroport. / I'm going to the airport.
Je vais à la bibliothèque. / I'm going to the library.
Je viens de l'aéroport. / I'm coming from the airport.
Je viens de la bibliothèque. / I'm coming from the library.

- With the preposition *à* (which combines to form *au* or *aux*) in front of the name of a country that is masculine.

  > *Nous allons au Canada.* / We're going to Canada.
  > *Janine vient aux États-Unis.* / Janine is coming to the United States.

  With the preposition *de* (which combines to form *du* or *des*) before the name of a country that is masculine.

  > *du Portugal* / from Portugal
  > *des Etats-Unis* / from the United States

  With the preposition *de* + a common noun to indicate possession.

  > *le livre du garçon* / the boy's book
  > *les livres des garçons* / the boys' books
  > *la robe de la jeune fille* / the girl's dress
  > *les poupées des petites filles* / the little girls' dolls

WITH CERTAIN EXPRESSIONS

- Indicating segments of the day.

  > *l'après-midi* / in the afternoon; *le matin* / in the morning; *le soir* / in the evening

- Common expressions.

  > *à l'école* / to school, in school; *à la maison* / at home
  > *la semaine dernière* / last week; *l'année dernière* / last year
  > *la plupart de* / most of
  > *la plupart des jeunes filles* / most of the girls

- As a partitive in the affirmative.

  > *J'ai du café.* / I have (some) coffee.
  > *Tu as de l'argent.* / You have (some) money.
  > *Il a des amis.* / He has friends.

Definite Article Not Used

However, the definite article is *not* used when the partitive is in the negative or when the definite article is used with an adjective.

> *Je n'ai pas de café.* / I haven't any coffee.
> *Tu n'as pas d'argent.* / You haven't any money.
> *Il a de bons amis.* / He has some good friends.

Do not use the definite article:

- In direct address: *Bonjour, docteur Leduc.*
- After the preposition *en: Nous écrivons en français.* Exceptions:

  en l'air / in the air; *en l'absence de* / in the absence of
  en l'honneur de / in honor of

- After the preposition *de* in an adjective phrase: *J'aime mon livre de français.*
- With a feminine country and continents when you use *en* / at, to or *de* / of, from.

  Je vais en France, en Angleterre, en Allemagne, en Australie, en Asie, et en Amérique.
  Paul vient de France, les Armstrong viennent d'Australie et Hilda vient d'Allemagne.

- With most cities: *à Paris, à New York; de Londres, de Montréal, de Sydney.*
- With a noun in apposition: *Paul, fils du professeur Leblanc, est très aimable.*
- With titles of monarchs:

  Louis Seize (Louis XVI) / Louis the Sixteenth

- With the preposition *sans* or with the construction *ne . . . ni . . . ni . . . :*

  Je n'ai ni papier ni stylo. / I have neither paper nor pen.
  Il est parti sans argent. / He left without money.

- With certain expressions of quantity that take *de: beaucoup de, trop de, combien de, peu de, plus de, assez de*
- With the preposition *avec* when the noun after it is abstract:

  Jean-Luc parle avec enthousiasme.

§3.2 INDEFINITE ARTICLE

The forms of the indefinite article are:

Singular
J'ai **un** *frère.* / I have a brother.
J'ai **une** *sœur.* / I have a sister.
Plural
J'ai **des** *frères.* / I have brothers.
J'ai **des** *sœurs.* / I have sisters.

The indefinite article is used:

- When you want to say "a" or "an." It is also used as a numeral to mean "one":

  un livre / a book or one book
  une orange / an orange or one orange

- In front of each noun in a series:

  J'ai un cahier, un crayon et une gomme. / I have a notebook, pencil, and eraser.

- With *C'est* or *Ce sont* with or without an adjective:

  C'est un docteur. / He's a doctor.
  C'est un mauvais docteur. / He's a bad doctor.
  Ce sont des étudiants. / They are students.

The indefinite article is *not* used:

- With *cent* and *mille:*

  J'ai cent dollars. / I have a hundred dollars.
  J'ai mille dollars. / I have a thousand dollars.

- With *il est, ils sont, elle est, elles sont* + an unmodified noun of nationality, profession, or religion:

  Elle est professeur. / She is a professor.
  Il est catholique. / He is (a) Catholic.

- When you use *quel* in an exclamation:

  Quelle femme! / What a woman!
  Quel homme! / What a man!

- With negations, particularly with the verb *avoir:*

  Avez-vous un livre? Non, je n'ai pas de livre. / Have you a book? No, I don't have a book (any book).

§3.3 PARTITIVE

The partitive denotes a *part* of a whole; in other words, some. In English, we express the partitive by saying some or any in front of the noun. Use the following forms in front of the noun:

Masculine singular: *du* or *de l'*
Feminine singular: *de la* or *de l'*
Masculine or feminine plural: *des*

Simple Affirmative

J'ai **du** café. / I have some coffee.
J'ai **de la** viande. / I have some meat.
J'ai **de l'**eau. / I have some water.
J'ai **des** bonbons. / I have some candy.

Simple Negative

Je n'ai **pas de** café. / I don't have any coffee.
Je n'ai **pas de** viande. / I don't have any meat.
Je n'ai **pas d'**eau. / I don't have any water.
Je n'ai **pas de** bonbons. / I don't have any candy.

With an Adjective

J'ai **de jolis** chapeaux. / I have some pretty hats.
J'ai **de jolies** robes. / I have some pretty dresses.

Note the following:
- When the noun is preceded by an adverb or noun of quantity or measure, use de, as in J'ai beaucoup de choses. / I have many things.
- When the noun is modified by another noun, use de, as in une école de filles.
- The partitive is not used with sans or ne . . . ni . . . ni.

  EXAMPLE:
  J'ai quitté la maison sans argent. / I left the house without any money.

- Use quelques and not the partitive when by "some" you mean "a few," in other words, "not many."

  EXAMPLES:
  J'ai quelques amis. / I have a few (some) friends.
  J'ai quelques bonbons. / I have a few (some) candies.

- When the negated verb is ne . . . que / only, the partitive consists of de plus the definite article.

  EXAMPLES:
  Elle ne lit que des livres. / She reads only books.
  Elle ne mange que des bonbons. / She eats only candy.

- The partitive must be repeated before each noun.

  EXAMPLE:
  Ici on vend du papier, de l'encre et des cahiers. / Here they sell paper, ink, and notebooks.

§4.

Nouns

§4.1
GENDER

A *noun* is a word that refers to a person, place, thing, or quality. Nouns are either masculine or feminine and require the article *le, la, l'*, or *les*. The gender of nouns that refer to persons or animals is obvious.

Examples

PERSONS		ANIMALS	
Masculine	**Feminine**	**Masculine**	**Feminine**
l'homme / the man	*la femme* / the woman	*le taureau* / the bull	*la vache* / the cow
le garçon / the boy	*la jeune fille* / the girl	*le coq* / the rooster	*la poule* / the hen
l'oncle / the uncle	*la tante* / the aunt	*le chat* / the cat	*la chatte* / the cat

- The gender of nouns referring to anything other than persons or animals must be learned with the noun.

Examples

Gender	Noun Endings	Examples
Masculine	*-age* or *-âge*	*l'âge* / age
		le fromage / cheese
	-ment	*le logement* / lodging
		le médicament / medicine (you take)
	-eau	*le chapeau* / hat
		le gâteau / cake
Feminine	*-ance*	*la circonstance* / circumstance
		la chance / chance, luck
	-ence	*l'apparence* / appearance
		la science / science
	-tion	*l'attention* / attention
		la notion / idea, notion
	-ette	*la fourchette* / fork
		la serviette / napkin
		la sucette / lollipop

Special Cases

	Masculine	Feminine
Some nouns have one meaning when masculine, another meaning when feminine.	*le livre* / book	*la livre* / pound
	le tour / turn	*la tour* / tower
Some nouns are the same for both.	*un élève* / pupil (boy)	*une élève* / pupil (girl)
	un enfant / child (boy)	*une enfant* / child (girl)
Some nouns add -e to the masculine to form the feminine.	*un cousin* / cousin	*une cousine* / cousin
	un ami / friend	*une amie* / friend
Some nouns change the *-eur* masculine ending to *-euse* for the feminine.	*un vendeur* / salesman	*une vendeuse* / saleswoman
	un menteur / liar	*une menteuse* / liar

§4.2 PLURAL OF NOUNS — THE BASICS

Add -s to the singular:

Singular	Plural
le livre / the book	*les livres* / the books
la maison / the house	*les maisons* / the houses
l'étudiant / the student	*les étudiants* / the students

If a noun ends in -s, -x, or -z in the singular, leave it alone:

Singular	Plural
le bras / the arm	*les bras* / the arms
la voix / the voice	*les voix* / the voices
le nez / the nose	*les nez* / the noses

If a noun ends in -al in the singular, change -al to -aux:

Singular
le journal / the newspaper

Plural
les journaux / the newspapers

If a noun ends in -eu or -eau in the singular, add -x:

Singular
le feu / the fire
le bureau / the office, the desk

Plural
les feux / the fires
les bureaux / the offices, desks

Common irregular nouns

Singular	Plural
le ciel / the sky	*les cieux* / the skies
l'œil / the eye	*les yeux* / the eyes

§5.

Adjectives

§5.1 FORMATION

Feminine Singular

- The feminine singular of an adjective is normally formed by adding -e to the masculine singular.

  EXAMPLES

  joli — jolie / pretty   *présent — présente* / present
  grand — grande / tall

- If a masculine singular adjective already ends in -e, the feminine singular is the same form.

  EXAMPLES

  aimable / kind   *énorme* / huge   *faible* / weak

- Some feminine singular forms are irregular. If a masculine singular adjective ends in -c, change it to -que for the feminine; -er to -ère; -g to gue; and -x to -se.

  EXAMPLES

  public — publique / public   *long — longue* / long
  premier — première / first   *heureux — heureuse* / happy
  actif — active / active

- Some masculine singular adjectives double the final consonant before adding -e to form the feminine.

  EXAMPLES

  ancien — ancienne / old   *cruel — cruelle* / cruel
  bas — basse / low   *gentil — gentille* / kind, nice
  bon — bonne / good

- The following feminine singular adjectives are formed from the irregular masculine singular forms:

Masculine Singular Before a Masculine Singular Noun Beginning with a Consonant	Irregular Masculine Singular Before a Masculine Singular Noun Beginning with a Vowel or Silent *H*	Feminine Singular
beau / beautiful, handsome	*bel ami*	*belle amie*
fou / crazy	*fol ami*	*folle amie*
nouveau / new	*nouvel hôtel*	*nouvelle amie*
vieux / old	*vieil ami*	*vieille amie*

> | Mnemonic tip | *La vieille dame a passé la veille de Noël avec son vieil ami dans un vieux cabaret.* / The old lady spent Christmas Eve with her old friend in an old cabaret.

- Some common masculine singular adjectives have irregular forms in the feminine singular. These do not fall into any particular category like those above.

    EXAMPLES

    blanc — blanche / white
    complet — complète / complete
    doux — douce / soft, smooth, sweet
    faux — fausse / false

    favori — favorite / favorite
    frais — fraîche / fresh
    sec — sèche / dry

Plural

- The plural is normally formed by adding *-s* to the masculine or feminine singular.

    EXAMPLES

    bon — bons; bonne — bonnes / good
    joli — jolis; jolie — jolies / pretty

- If the masculine singular already ends in *-s* or *-x*, it remains the same in the masculine plural.

    EXAMPLES

    gris — gris / gray   *heureux — heureux* / happy

- If a masculine singular adjective ends in *-al*, it changes to *-aux* (with some exceptions).

    EXAMPLES

    égal — égaux / equal   *principal — principaux* / principal

- If a masculine singular adjective ends in *-eau*, it changes to *-eaux*.

    EXAMPLE

    nouveau — nouveaux / new

§5.2 AGREEMENT

An adjective agrees in gender (feminine or masculine) and number (singular or plural) with the noun or pronoun it modifies.

EXAMPLES:

Alexandre et Théodore sont beaux et intelligents. / Alexander and Theodore are handsome and smart.
Yolande est belle. / Yolande is beautiful.
Janine et Monique sont belles. / Janine and Monique are beautiful.

Hélène et Simone sont actives. / Helene and Simone are active.
Anne est jolie. / Anne is pretty.
C'est un bel arbre. / It is a beautiful tree.
Ils sont amusants. / They are amusing.
Chaque garçon est présent. / Every boy is here (present).
Chaque jeune fille est présente. / Every girl is here (present).
Valentine est absente. / Valentine is absent.

§5.3 POSITION

- In French, most descriptive adjectives are placed after the noun; e.g., colors, nationality, religion: *une robe blanche* / a white dress, *un fromage français* / a French cheese, *une femme catholique* / a Catholic woman
  Remember: A noun indicating nationality is capitalized.

  un Américain / an American (male), *une Américaine* / an American (female), *un Français* / a French man, *une Française* / a French woman

- Here are some examples of common short adjectives that are generally placed in front of the noun:

  un autre livre / another book, *un bel arbre* / a beautiful tree, *un beau cadeau* / a beautiful gift, *un bon dîner* / a good dinner, *chaque jour* / each day, *un gros livre* / a big book, *une jeune dame* / a young lady, *une jolie maison* / a pretty house, *une petite table* / a small table, *plusieurs amis* / several friends, *un vieil homme* / an old man, *le premier rang* / the first row, *quelques bonbons* / some candy, *un tel garçon* / such a boy, *toute la journée* / all day.

- Some adjectives change in meaning, depending on whether the adjective is in front of the noun or after it. The most common are:

la semaine dernière / last week	*la dernière semaine* / the last (final) week
ma robe propre / my clean dress	*ma propre robe* / my own dress
une femme brave / a brave woman	*une brave femme* / a fine woman
le même moment / the same moment	*le moment même* / the very moment
un livre cher / an expensive book	*un cher ami* / a dear friend

§5.4
TYPES

§5.4–1
Descriptive

A descriptive adjective is a word that describes a noun or pronoun: *une belle maison* / a beautiful house, *un beau livre* / a beautiful book, *un bel arbre* / a beautiful tree, *une jolie femme* / a pretty woman.

> *Elle est grande.* / She is tall.

§5.4–2
Demonstrative

A demonstrative adjective is used to point out something or someone.

Gender	Singular	Plural
Masculine	*ce, cet* / this, that	*ces* / these, those
Feminine	*cette* / this, that	*ces* / these, those

EXAMPLES:
Ce garçon est beau. / This boy is handsome.
Cet arbre est beau. / This tree is beautiful.
Cette femme est belle. / This woman is beautiful.
Ces hommes sont beaux. / These men are handsome.
Ces livres sont beaux. / These books are beautiful.
Ces dames sont belles. / These ladies are beautiful.

If you wish to make a contrast between "this" and "that" or "these" and "those," add *-ci* this, these or *-là* that, those to the noun with a hyphen.

> *Ce garçon-ci est plus fort que ce garçon-là.* / This boy is stronger than that boy.

The form *cet* is used in front of a masculine singular noun or adjective beginning with a vowel or silent *h: cet arbre, cet homme.*

If there is more than one noun, a demonstrative adjective must be used in front of each noun: *cette dame et ce monsieur.*

§5.4–3
Interrogative

The adjective *quel* is generally regarded as interrogative because it is frequently used in a question. Its forms are *quel, quelle, quels, quelles.*

EXAMPLES:
Quel livre voulez-vous? / Which book do you want?
Quel est votre nom? / What is your name?

Quelle heure est-il? / What time is it?
Quelle est votre adresse? / What is your address?
Quels sont les mois de l'année? / What are the months of the year?
Quelles sont les saisons? / What are the seasons?

The adjective *quel* is also used in exclamations. Note that the indefinite article *un (une)* is not used in this case.

EXAMPLES

Quel garçon! / What a boy!
Quelle jeune fille! / What a girl!

§5.4 – 4
Possessive

MASCULINE	
Singular	**Plural**
mon livre / my book	*mes livres* / my books
ton stylo / your pen	*tes stylos* / your pens
son ballon / his (her, its) balloon	*ses ballons* / his (her, its) balloons
notre parapluie / our umbrella	*nos parapluies* / our umbrellas
votre sandwich / your sandwich	*vos sandwichs* / your sandwiches
leur gâteau / their cake	*leurs gâteaux* / their cakes

FEMININE	
Singular	**Plural**
ma robe / my dress	*mes robes* / my dresses
ta jaquette / your jacket	*tes jaquettes* / your jackets
sa balle / his (her, its) ball	*ses balles* / his (her, its) balls
notre maison / our house	*nos maisons* / our houses
votre voiture / your car	*vos voitures* / your cars
leur sœur / their sister	*leurs sœurs* / their sisters

- A possessive adjective agrees in gender and number with the noun it modifies.

- *Notre, votre,* and *leur* do not agree with the gender of the noun in the singular. They are all the same, whether in front of a masculine or feminine singular noun.

- Some possessive adjectives do not agree with the gender of the noun in the plural. They are all the same, whether in front of a masculine or feminine plural noun: *mes, tes, ses, nos, vos, leurs.*

- Be aware of *mon (ma), ton (ta), son (sa):* In front of a feminine singular noun beginning with a vowel or silent *h,* the masculine singular forms are used: *mon, ton, son* — not *ma, ta, sa.*

> *mon adresse* / my address
> *ton opinion* / your opinion
> *son amie* / his (or her) friend
> *mon habitude* / my habit (custom)

- Since *son, sa,* and *ses* can mean "his" or "her," you may add *à lui* or *à elle* to make the meaning clear.

> *sa maison à lui* / his house
> *sa maison à elle* / her house
> *son livre à lui* / his book
> *son livre à elle* / her book
> *ses livres à lui* / his books
> *ses livres à elle* / her books

- If there is more than one noun, a possessive adjective must be used in front of each noun: *ma mère et mon père, mon livre et mon cahier.*

Possessive Adjectives with Parts of the Body and Clothing

- When using the verb *avoir,* the definite article is normally used with parts of the body, **not** the possessive adjective.

  Henri a les mains sales. / Henry has dirty hands.
  Simone a les cheveux roux. / Simone has red hair.

- When using a reflexive verb, the definite article is normally used, **not** the possessive adjective.

  Paulette s'est lavé les cheveux. / Paulette washed her hair.

- The *definite article* is used instead of the possessive adjective when referring to parts of the body or clothing if it is clear who the possessor is.

  Henri tient le livre dans la main. / Henry is holding the book in his hand.

§5.4 – 5
Comparative and Superlative

Comparative

Of the same degree: *aussi . . . que* / as . . .as
Of a lesser degree: *moins . . . que* / less . . . than
Of a higher degree: *plus . . . que* / more . . . than

> *Janine est aussi grande que Monique.* / Janine is as tall as Monique.
>
> *Monique est moins intelligente que Janine.* / Monique is less intelligent than Janine.
>
> *Janine est plus jolie que Monique.* / Janine is prettier than Monique.

• *Aussi . . . que* becomes *si . . . que* in a negative sentence.

> *Robert n'est pas si grand que Joseph.* / Robert is not as tall as Joseph.

The comparative forms of the adjective "bad" are *mauvais, pire, le pire.*

> *Ce crayon est mauvais.* / This pencil is bad.
>
> *Ce crayon est pire que l'autre.* / This pencil is worse than the other.
>
> *Ce crayon est le pire.* / This pencil is the worst.

• *Plus que* / more than becomes *plus de* + a number.

EXAMPLES

> *Il a plus de cinquante ans.* / He is more than fifty years old.
>
> *Je lui ai donné plus de cent dollars.* / I gave him (her) more than a hundred dollars.

Superlative

• The superlative is formed by placing the appropriate definite article *(le, la, les)* in front of the comparative:

> *Marie est la plus jolie jeune fille de la classe.* / Mary is the prettiest girl in the class.

• If the adjective normally follows the noun, the definite article must be used twice — in front of the noun and in front of the superlative:

> *Monsieur Hibou fut le président le plus sage de la nation.* / Mr. Hibou was the wisest president of the nation.

• After a superlative, the preposition *de* (not *dans*) is normally used to express "in":

> *Pierre est le plus beau garçon de la classe.* / Peter is the most handsome boy in the class.

- If more than one comparative or superlative is expressed, each is repeated:

> *Marie est la plus intelligente et la plus sérieuse de l'école.* / Mary is the most intelligent and most serious in the school.

Une devinette (a riddle) using a superlative:

> *Quelle est la chose la plus sale de la maison?* / What is the dirtiest thing in the house?
>
> *un balai* / a broom

Irregular Comparative and Superlative Adjectives

Adjective (m)	Comparative	Superlative
bon / good	*meilleur* / better	*le meilleur* / (the) best
mauvais / bad	*plus mauvais* } worse *pire*	*le plus mauvais* } (the) worst *le pire*
petit / small	*plus petit* / smaller (in size)	*le plus petit* / (the) smallest
	moindre / less (in importance)	*le moindre* / (the) least

§5.4–6
Meilleur and *Mieux*

Meilleur is an adjective and must agree in gender and number with the noun or pronoun it modifies.

EXAMPLE

Cette pomme est bonne, cette pomme-là est meilleure que celle-ci et celle-là est la meilleure. / This apple is good, that apple is better than this one, and that one is the best.

Mieux is an adverb and does not change in form.

EXAMPLE

Marie chante bien, Anne chante mieux que Marie et Claire chante le mieux. / Mary sings well, Anne sings better than Mary, and Claire sings the best.

> **Mnemonic tip** The adverb *bien* / (well) and the adverb *mieux* / (better) both contain *ie.*

§5.4–7
Adjectives Used in an Adverbial Sense

An adjective used as an adverb does not normally change in form.

Cette rose sent bon. / This rose smells good.
Ces bonbons coûtent cher. / These candies are expensive.

§6.

Pronouns

§6.1
TYPES

§6.1−1
Subject
Pronouns

The subject pronouns are:

Person	Singular	Plural
1st	*je (j')* / I	*nous* / we
2d	*tu* / you (familiar)	*vous* / you (singular polite or plural)
	il / he, it	
3d	*elle* / she, it	*ils* / they (m.)
	on / one	*elles* / they (f.)

- Note that *je* becomes *j'* before a vowel or a silent *h:*

  j'aime / I love; *j'hésite* / I hesitate.

- Remember that *vous* is not always plural; it is also the polite form of the second person; *tu* is the familiar form. You can use the *tu* form with members of the family and close friends, but always use the *vous* form with strangers and with people you do not know well.

The direct object pronouns are:

§6.1−2
Direct Object
Pronouns

Person	Singular	Plural
1st	*me (m')* / me	*nous* / us
2d	*te (t')* / you (familiar)	*vous* / you (singular polite or plural)
3d	$\begin{cases} \textit{le (l')} \text{ / him, it} \\ \textit{la (l')} \text{ / her, it} \end{cases}$ (person or thing)	*les* / them (persons or things)

- A direct object pronoun takes the place of a direct object noun.

- A direct object noun ordinarily comes after the verb, but a direct object pronoun is ordinarily placed *in front* of the verb or infinitive.

36

EXAMPLES

J'ai les lettres. / I have the letters. → *Je les ai.* / I have them.
Je connais Luigi. / I know Luigi. → *Je le connais.* / I know him.

> | Mnemonic tip | *Je lis la leçon.* / I'm reading the lesson.
> Drop the noun *leçon;* what remains is *la*, the feminine singular definite article. It now becomes the direct object pronoun. Place it in front of the verb: *Je la lis.* / I'm reading it.

- *Me, te, le,* and *la* become *m', t', l'* when directly followed by a verb that starts with a vowel or silent *h.*

§6.1–3
Indirect Object Pronouns

The indirect object pronouns are:

Person	Singular		Plural	
1st	*me (m')*	to me	*nous*	to us
2d	*te (t')*	to you (familiar)	*vous*	to you (singular polite or plural)
3d	*lui*	to him, to her	*leur*	to them

- An indirect object pronoun takes the place of an indirect object noun.

- An indirect object pronoun is ordinarily placed *in front* of the verb.

  EXAMPLES

  Je parle à Janine. / I'm talking to Janine. → *Je lui parle.* / I'm talking to her.
  Je parle à Luigi et à mon ami. / I'm talking to Luigi and my friend. → *Je leur parle.* / I'm talking to them.

§6.1–4
Double Object Pronouns

To get a picture of what the word order is when you have more than one object pronoun (direct and indirect) in a sentence, see Word Order of Elements in French Sentences, §11.

§6.1–5
En

- The pronoun *en* takes the place of the partitive and serves as a direct object. It can refer to persons or things.

  EXAMPLES

  Avez-vous des frères? / Do you have any brothers?
  Oui, j'en ai. / Yes, I have (some).

Avez-vous de l'argent? / Have you any money?
Oui, j'en ai. / Yes, I have (some). *Non, je n'en ai pas.* / No, I don't have any.

- The past participle of a compound verb does not agree with the preceding direct object *en.*

  Avez-vous écrit des lettres? / Did you write any letters?
  Oui, j'en ai écrit trois. / Yes, I wrote three (of them).

- When using a reflexive verb, use *en* to take the place of the preposition *de* + a thing.

  Est-ce que vous vous souvenez de l'adresse? / Do you remember the address?
  Oui, je m'en souviens. / Yes, I remember it.

  Est-ce que vous prenez des hors-d'œuvre? / Are you helping yourself to the hors d'œuvre?
  Oui, merci, j'en prends. / Yes, thank you, I'm helping myself to some.

  Do not use *en* to take the place of the preposition *de* + a person. Use a disjunctive pronoun (see §6.1–7).

  Est-ce que vous vous souvenez de cette dame? / Do you remember this lady?
  Oui, je me souviens d'elle. / Yes, I remember her.

- Use *en* to take the place of *de* + noun and retain the word of quantity.

  Avez-vous beaucoup d'amis? / Do you have many friends?
  Oui, j'en ai beaucoup. / Yes, I have many (of them).

  Madame Paquet a-t-elle mis trop de sel dans le ragoût? / Did Mrs. Paquet put too much salt in the stew?
  Oui, elle en a mis trop dans le ragoût. / Yes, she put too much (of it) in the stew.

- Use *en* to take the place of the preposition *de* + the place to mean "from there."

  Est-ce que vous venez de l'école? / Are you coming from school?
  Oui, j'en viens. / Yes, I'm coming from there.
  Non, je n'en viens pas. / No, I am not coming from there.

§6.1–6
Y

Use *y* as a pronoun to serve as an object replacing a prepositional phrase beginning with *à, dans, sur,* or *chez* that refers to things, places, or ideas.

Est-ce que vous pensez à l'examen? / **Are you thinking of the exam?**

Oui, j'y pense. / **Yes, I'm (thinking of it).**

Je réponds à la lettre. / **I'm answering the letter.**

J'y réponds. / **I'm answering it.**

Est-ce que les fleurs sont sur la table? / **Are the flowers on the table?**

Oui, elles y sont. / **Yes, they are (there).**

Est-ce que vous allez chez Pierre? / **Are you going to Pierre's?**

Oui, j'y vais. / **Yes, I'm going (there).**

§6.1–7 Disjunctive Pronouns

Person	Singular		Plural	
1st	*moi*	me, I	*nous*	us, we
2nd	*toi*	you (familiar)	*vous*	you (formal singular or plural)
3rd	*soi*	oneself		
	lui	him, he	*eux*	them, they (m.)
	elle	her, she	*elles*	them, they (f.)

> **Mnemonic tip**

Je vais chez moi. / **I'm going to my house.**
Tu vas chez toi. / **You're going to your house.**
Il va chez lui. / **He's going to his house.**
Elle va chez elle. / **She's going to her house.**
On va chez soi. / **One is going to one's own house.**

Nous allons chez nous. / **We're going to our house.**
Vous allez chez vous. / **You're going to your house.**
Ils vont chez eux. / **They're going to their house.**
Elles vont chez elles. / **They're going to their house.**

A disjunctive pronoun is used:

● as object of a preposition.

Elle parle avec moi. / **She is talking with me.**
Je pense toujours à toi. / **I always think of you.**

● in a compound subject or object.

Elle et lui sont amoureux. / **He and she are in love.**
Je vous connais—toi et lui. / **I know you—you and him.**

- for emphasis.

  Moi, je parle bien; lui, il ne parle pas bien. / I speak well; he does not speak well.

- to indicate possession with *à* if the verb is *être* and if the subject is a noun, personal pronoun, or demonstrative pronoun.

  Ce livre est à moi. / This book is mine.
  Je suis à toi. / I am yours.

- with *c'est*.

  Qui est à la porte? — C'est moi. / Who is at the door? It is I.
  C'est toi? Oui, c'est moi. / Is it you? Yes, it is I.

- with *ce sont* in a statement but not usually in a question.

  Est-ce que ce sont eux? — Oui, ce sont eux. / Is it they? — Yes, it's they.

- with *même* and *mêmes*.

  Est-ce Pierre? — Oui, c'est lui-même. / Is it Peter? Yes, it's he himself.
  Vont-ils les manger eux-mêmes? / Are they going to eat them themselves?

- when no verb is stated.

  Qui est à l'appareil? Moi. / Who is on the phone? I (am).
  Qui a brisé le vase? Eux. / Who broke the vase? They (did).

See also Order of Elements in French Sentences, §11.

§6.1–8
Demonstrative
Pronouns

The demonstrative pronouns are:

	Singular	**Plural**
Masculine	*celui* / the one	*ceux* / the ones
Feminine	*celle* / the one	*celles* / the ones

EXAMPLES
J'ai mangé mon gâteau et celui de Pierre. / I ate my cake and Peter's.
Il aime beaucoup ma voiture et celle de Jacques. / He likes my car very much and Jack's.

J'ai mangé mes petits pois et ceux de David. / I ate my peas and David's.

J'aime tes jupes et celles de Jeanne. / I like your skirts and Joan's.

J'ai deux éclairs; est-ce que tu préfères celui-ci ou celui-là? / I have two eclairs; do you prefer this one or that one?

J'ai deux pommes; est-ce que tu préfères celle-ci ou celle-là? / I have two apples; do you prefer this one or that one?

Une devinette / a riddle

J'ai un chapeau, mais je n'ai pas de tête. Ne trouvez-vous pas que c'est bête? / I have a hat, but I don't have a head. Don't you think it's stupid?

un champignon / a mushroom

---

ce (c'), ceci, cela, ça

These are demonstrative pronouns but they are invariable; that is, they do not change in gender and number. They refer to things that are not identified by name and may refer to an idea or a statement mentioned.

EXAMPLES

C'est vrai. / It's true.

Ceci est vrai. / This is true. *Ceci est faux.* / This is false.

Cela est vrai. / That is true. *Cela est faux.* / That is false.

Ça m'intéresse beaucoup. / That interests me very much.

Qu'est-ce que c'est que cela?   *Qu'est-ce que c'est que ça?* / What's that?

Note that *cela* shortens to *ça*.

§6.1–9 Indefinite Pronouns

aucun (aucune) / not any, not one, none

un autre (une autre) / another, another one

nous autres Français / we French (people)

nous autres Américains / we American (people)

certains (certaines) / certain ones

chacun (chacune) / each one

nul (nulle) / not one, not any, none

n'importe qui, n'importe quel / anyone

n'importe quoi / anything

on / people, one, they, you, we

On dit qu'il va pleuvoir. / They say that it's going to rain.

personne / no one, nobody

plusieurs / several

> *J'en ai plusieurs.* / I have several (of them).

quelque chose / something
quelqu'un (quelqu'une) / someone, somebody
quelques-uns (quelques-unes) / some, a few
quiconque / whoever, whosoever
soi / oneself

> *On est chez soi dans cet hôtel.* / People feel at home in this hotel.

tout / all, everything

> *Tout est bien qui finit bien.* / All is well that ends well.

§6.1 – 10 Interrogative Pronouns

Referring to Persons

- As subject of a verb:

> *Qui est à l'appareil?* / Who is on the phone?
> *Qui est-ce qui est à l'appareil?* / Who is on the phone?
> *Lequel des deux garçons arrive?* / Which (one) of the two boys is arriving?
> *Laquelle des deux jeunes filles est ici?* / Which (one) of the two girls is here?

- As direct object of a verb:

> *Qui aimez-vous?* / Whom do you love?
> *Qui est-ce que vous aimez?* / Whom do you love?
> *Lequel de ces deux garçons aimez-vous?* / Which (one) of these two boys do you love?
> *Laquelle de ces deux jeunes filles aimez-vous?* / Which (one) of these two girls do you love?

- As object of a preposition:

> *Avec qui allez-vous au cinéma?* / With whom are you going to the movies?
> *A qui parlez-vous au téléphone?* / To whom are you talking on the telephone?

Note that when the interrogative pronouns *lequel (laquelle)*, *lesquels (lesquelles)* are objects of the prepositions *à* or *de*, their forms are:

Singular	Plural
auquel (à laquelle)	*auxquels (auxquelles)*
duquel (de laquelle)	*desquels (desquelles)*

Auquel de ces deux garçons parlez-vous? / **To which (one) of these two boys are you talking?**

A laquelle de ces deux jeunes filles parlez-vous? / **To which (one) of these two girls are you talking?**

Auxquels de ces hommes parlez-vous? / **To which (ones) of these men do you talk?**

Auxquelles de ces femmes parlez-vous? / **To which (ones) of these women are you talking?**

Duquel de ces deux garçons parlez-vous? / **About which (one) of these two boys are you talking?**

Referring to Things

- As subject of a verb:

Qu'est-ce qui est arrivé? / **What arrived? OR What happened?**
Qu'est-ce qui s'est passé? / **What happened?**

Une devinette avec qu'est-ce qui

Qu'est-ce qui vous appartient et dont les autres se servent souvent? / **What belongs to you that others use often?**

votre nom / **your name**

Laquelle de ces deux voitures marche bien? / **Which (one) of these two cars runs well?**
Lesquels de tous ces trains sont modernes? / **Which (ones) of all these trains are modern?**

- As direct object of a verb:

Que faites-vous? / **What are you doing?**
Qu'a-t-elle? / **What does she have? OR What's the matter with her?**
Qu'est-ce que vous faites? / **What are you doing?**
Laquelle de ces voitures préférez-vous? / **Which (one) of these cars do you prefer?**

- As object of a preposition:

Avec quoi écrivez-vous? / **With what are you writing?**
A quoi pensez-vous? / **Of what are you thinkng? OR What are you thinking of?**

§6.1–11 Possessive Pronouns

MASCULINE			
Singular		**Plural**	
le mien	mine	les miens	mine
le tien	yours (familiar)	les tiens	yours (familiar)
le sien	his, hers, its	les siens	his, hers, its
le nôtre	ours	les nôtres	ours
le vôtre	yours	les vôtres	yours
le leur	theirs	les leurs	theirs

FEMININE			
Singular		**Plural**	
la mienne	mine	les miennes	mine
la tienne	yours (familiar)	les tiennes	yours (familiar)
la sienne	his, hers, its	les siennes	his, hers, its
la nôtre	ours	les nôtres	ours
la vôtre	yours	les vôtres	yours
la leur	theirs	les leurs	theirs

- A possessive pronoun takes the place of a possessive adjective + noun.

  mon livre / my book; *le mien* / mine.

- A possessive pronoun agrees in gender and number with what it is replacing.

  son livre / his (her) book; *le sien* / his (hers).

- When the definite articles *le* and *les* are preceded by the prepositions *à* and *de,* they combine as follows: *au mien, aux miens, du mien, des miens.*

  Paul me parle de ses parents et je lui parle des miens. / Paul is talking to me about his parents and I am talking to him about mine.
  Je préfère ma voiture à la tienne. / I prefer my car to yours.

- Possessive pronouns are used with *être* to emphasize a distinction.

  Ce livre-ci est le mien et celui-là est le tien. / This book is mine and that one is yours.

- If no distinction is made as to who owns what, use *être* + *à* + disjunctive pronoun.

  Ce livre est à lui. / This book is his.

- Instead of using the possessive pronouns in French, we say "one of my friends," "one of my books," etc.

  un de mes amis / a friend of mine; *un de mes livres* / a book of mine

  une de ses amies / a girlfriend of his (hers)
  un de nos amis / a friend of ours

§6.1–12 Reflexive Pronouns

- The reflexive pronouns, which are used with reflexive verbs, are *me, te, se, nous,* and *vous.*

- The corresponding English pronouns are: myself, yourself, herself, himself, oneself, itself, ourselves, yourselves, themselves.

- To form the present tense of a reflexive verb in a simple affirmative sentence, put the reflexive pronoun in front of the verb.

  Je me lave. / I wash myself.

- A reflexive verb expresses an action that turns back upon the subject.

  Jacqueline se lave tous les jours. / Jacqueline washes herself every day.

You must be careful to use the appropriate reflexive pronoun—the one that matches the subject pronoun. You already know the subject pronouns, but here they are again, beside the reflexive pronouns.

Person	Singular	Plural
1st	*je me lave*	*nous nous lavons*
2d	*tu te laves*	*vous vous lavez*
3d	*il se lave* *elle se lave* *on se lave*	*ils se lavent* *elles se lavent*

To get a picture of what the word order is when you have more than one pronoun of any kind in a sentence, see Word Order of Elements in French Sentences (§11.).

§6.1–13 Relative Pronouns

A *relative pronoun* is a word that refers to an antecedent. An *antecedent* is something that comes before something; it can be a word, a phrase, a clause that is replaced by a pronoun or some other substitute. For example, in the sentence "Is it Mary who did that?" "who" is the relative pronoun and "Mary" is the antecedent. Another example: "It seems to me that you are wrong, which is what I had suspected right along." The relative pronoun is "which" and the antecedent is the clause, "that you are wrong."

Some common relative pronouns are:

- *dont* / of whom, of which, whose, whom, which

    Voici le livre dont j'ai besoin. / Here is the book (that) I need.
    Monsieur Béry, dont le fils est avocat, est maintenant en France. / Mr. Béry, whose son is a lawyer, is now in France.

- *ce dont* / what, of which, that of which

    Je ne trouve pas ce dont j'ai besoin. / I don't find what I need.
    Ce dont vous parlez est absurde. / What you are talking about is absurd.

- *ce que (ce qu')* / what, that which

    Comprenez-vous ce que je vous dis? / Do you understand what I am telling you?
    Comprenez-vous ce qu'elle vous dit? / Do you understand what she is saying to you?
    Je comprends ce que vous dites et je comprends ce qu'elle dit. / I understand what you are saying and I understand what she is saying.

- *ce qui* / what, that which

    Ce qui est vrai est vrai. / What is true is true.
    Je ne sais pas ce qui s'est passé. / I don't know what happened.

    Note that *ce qui* is a subject.

- *lequel* (in all its forms) / which

    As a relative pronoun, *lequel* (in its various forms) is used as object of a preposition referring to things.

    Donnez-moi un autre morceau de papier sur lequel je peux écrire mon adresse. / Give me another piece of paper on which I can write my address.

- *où* / where, in which, on which

  > *Aimez-vous la salle à manger où nous mangeons?* / Do you like the dining room where we eat?
  > *Je vais ouvrir le tiroir où j'ai mis l'argent.* / I am going to open the drawer where I put the money.

- *que* or *qu'* / whom, which, that

  > *Le garçon que vous voyez là-bas est mon meilleur ami.* / The boy whom you see over there is my best friend.
  > *La composition qu'elle a écrite est excellente.* / The composition (that) she wrote is excellent.

- *qui* / who, whom, which, that

  > *Connais-tu la jeune fille qui parle avec mon frère?* / Do you know the girl who is talking with my brother?
  > *Avez-vous une bicyclette qui marche bien?* / Do you have a bicycle that (which) runs well?

§6.1 – 14
C'est + adjective + *à* + infinitive

C'EST + ADJECTIVE + À + INFINITIVE

C'est difficile à faire. / It is difficult to do.

Use this construction when what is being referred to *has already been mentioned.*

EXAMPLES
Le devoir pour demain est difficile, n'est-ce pas? / The homework for tomorrow is difficult, isn't it?
Oui, c'est difficile à faire. / Yes, it [the homework] is difficult to do.

J'aimerais faire une blouse. / I would like to make a blouse.
C'est facile à faire! Je vais vous montrer. / It's easy to do! I'll show you.

Il est + adjective + *de* + infinitive

IL EST + ADJECTIVE + DE + INFINITIVE

> *Il est impossible de lire ce gros livre en une heure.* / It is impossible to read this thick book within one hour.

Use this construction when the thing that is impossible, or difficult, or easy (or any adjective) to do is mentioned in the same sentence at the same time.

§6.1–15
Neuter
Pronoun *le*

The word *le* is the masculine singular definite article. It is also the masculine singular direct object. *Le* is used as a neuter pronoun and functions as a direct object referring to an adjective, a phrase, a clause, or a complete statement. It is generally not translated into English, except to mean "it" or "so."

> *Janine est jolie, mais Henriette ne l'est pas.* / Janine is pretty, but Henrietta isn't.
> *Moi, je crois qu'ils vont gagner le match, et vous? Je le crois aussi.* / I think they are going to win the game, and you? I think so too.

To get a picture of what the word order is when you have more than one pronoun of any kind in a sentence, see Word Order of Elements in French Sentences, §11.

§7.

Verbs

SUBJECT AND VERB

A subject and its corresponding verb form must agree in *person* (first, second, or third) and number (singular or plural).

EXAMPLE:
Je vais au cinéma. / I'm going to the movies.

SUBJECT AND REFLEXIVE PRONOUN OF A REFLEXIVE VERB

A subject and reflexive pronoun must agree in person and number.

EXAMPLE
Je me lave tous les matins. / I wash myself every morning.

SUBJECT AND PAST PARTICIPLE OF AN *ÊTRE* VERB

The past participle of an *être* verb agrees with the subject in gender and number.

Elle est allée au cinéma. / She went to the movies. OR She has gone to the movies.
Elles sont allées au cinéma. / They went to the movies. OR They have gone to the movies.

PRECEDING REFLEXIVE PRONOUN AND PAST PARTICIPLE OF A REFLEXIVE VERB

Elle s'est lavée. / She washed herself.
Elles se sont lavées. / They washed themselves.

However, there is *no* agreement made with the past participle of a reflexive verb if the reflexive pronoun serves as an indirect object pronoun. In the following example, *se (s')* is the indirect object; *les mains* the direct object.

Elle s'est lavé les mains. / She washed her hands.
Elles se sont lavé les mains. / They washed their hands.

Note this:

Elles se sont regardées. / They looked at each other.

49

Here, the reflexive pronoun *se* serves as the direct object. How do you know? There is no other obvious direct object mentioned, so what they looked at was *se* (each other); of course, you have to look at the subject to see what the gender and number is of the reflexive pronoun *se* in the sentence you are dealing with. The action of the verb is reciprocal.

Remember that the verb *regarder* in French means "to look at" in English; the preposition "at" is not expressed with *à* in French; it is included in the verb — that is why we are dealing with the reflexive pronoun as a direct object here, not an indirect object pronoun.

This same sentence, *Elles se sont regardées,* might also mean: "They looked at themselves." The principle of agreement is still the same. If you mean to say "They looked at each other," in order to avoid two meanings, add *l'une et l'autre.* If more than two persons, add *les unes les autres.*

And note:

Elles se sont parlé au téléphone. / They talked to each other on the telephone.

Here, the reflexive pronoun *se* is the indirect object because they spoke to each other; *parler à* is what you are dealing with here. And remember that no agreement is made on a past participle with an indirect object. The action of the verb is reciprocal.

PAST PARTICIPLE OF AN *AVOIR* VERB WITH A PRECEDING DIRECT OBJECT

EXAMPLES
Je l'ai vue au concert. / I saw her at the concert.

- There is agreement on the past participle *(vue)* because the preceding direct object is *la (l').* Agreement is made in gender and number.

Aimez-vous les fleurs que je vous ai données? / Do you like the flowers (that) I gave you?

- There is agreement on the past participle *(données)* of this *avoir* verb because there is a preceding direct object, *les fleurs;* the relative pronoun *que* refers to *les fleurs.* Since this direct object noun precedes the verb, the past participle must agree in gender and number. A preceding direct object, therefore, can be a pronoun or noun.

Quels films avez-vous vus? / What films did you see?

- There is agreement on the past participle *(vus)* of this *avoir* verb because the preceding direct object, *films,* is a masculine plural noun.

Avez-vous mangé les pâtisseries? / Did you eat the.pastries?
Oui, je les ai mangées. / Yes, I ate them.

- In the response to this question, there is agreement on the past participle *(mangées)* of this *avoir* verb because the preceding direct object, *les,* refers to *les pâtisseries,* a feminine plural noun.

J'en ai mangé assez. / I ate enough (of them).

- There is no agreement on the past participle *(mangé)* of this *avoir* verb because the preceding direct object is, in this sentence, the pronoun *en.* We do not normally make an agreement with *en,* whether it precedes or follows. This is an exception.

§7.2 PAST PARTICIPLE

REGULAR FORMATION

Infinitive	Type Ending	Drop	Add	Past Participle
donner	-er	-er	é	*donné*
finir	-ir	-ir	i	*fini*
vendre	-re	-re	u	*vendu*

COMMON IRREGULAR PAST PARTICIPLES

Infinitive	Past Participle
apprendre	appris
asseoir	assis
avoir	eu
boire	bu
comprendre	compris
conduire	conduit
connaître	connu
construire	construit
courir	couru
couvrir	couvert
craindre	craint
croire	cru
devenir	devenu
devoir	dû
dire	dit
écrire	écrit
être	été
faire	fait
falloir	fallu
lire	lu
mettre	mis
mourir	mort
naître	né
offrir	offert
ouvrir	ouvert
paraître	paru
permettre	permis
plaire	plu
pleuvoir	plu
pouvoir	pu
prendre	pris
promettre	promis
recevoir	reçu
revenir	revenu
rire	ri
savoir	su
suivre	suivi
taire	tu
tenir	tenu
valoir	valu
venir	venu
vivre	vécu
voir	vu
vouloir	voulu

§7.3 TYPES

§7.3–1 Auxiliary Verbs *avoir* and *être*

The auxiliary (helping) verbs *avoir* and *être* are used in any of the seven simple tenses + the past participle of the main verb you are using to form any of the compound tenses. You must be careful to choose the proper helping verb with the main verb. Some verbs take *avoir* and some take *être* to form the compound tenses.

- Most French verbs are conjugated with *avoir* to form a compound tense.
- All reflexive verbs, such as *se laver,* are conjugated with *être.*

The following is a list of common nonreflexive verbs that are conjugated with *être.*

1. *aller* to go   *Elle est allée au cinéma.*
2. *arriver* to arrive *Elle est arrivée.*
3. **descendre* to go down, come down   *Elle est descendue vite. |* She came down quickly. BUT: **Elle a descendu la valise. |* She brought down the suitcase.
4. *devenir* to become *Elle est devenue folle.*
5. *entrer* to enter, go in, come in   *Elle est entrée.*
6. **monter* to go up, come up   *Elle est montée lentement. |* She went up slowly. BUT: **Elle a monté l'escalier. |* She went up the stairs.
7. *mourir* to die   *Elle est morte.*
8. *naître* to be born *Elle est née le premier octobre.*
9. *partir* to leave   *Elle est partie.*
10. **passer* to go by, pass by   *Elle est passée par chez moi. |* She came by my house.

BUT: **Elle m'a passé le sel. |* She passed me the salt. AND: **Elle a passé un examen. |* She took an exam.
11. **rentrer* to go in again; to return (home)   *Elle est rentrée tôt. |* She returned home early. BUT: **Elle a rentré le chat dans la maison. |* She brought (took) the cat into the house.
12. *rester* to remain, stay   *Elle est restée chez elle.*
13. *retourner* to return, go back   *Elle est retournée*
14. *revenir* to come back   *Elle est revenue.*
15. **sortir* to go out *Elle est sortie hier soir. |* She went out last night. BUT: **Elle a sorti son mouchoir. |* She took out her handkerchief.
16. *tomber* to fall   *Elle est tombée.*
17. *venir* to come   *Elle est venue.*

* Some of these verbs, as noted above, are conjugated with *avoir* if the verb is used in a transitive sense and has a direct object.

§7.3–2 Transitive Verbs

A transitive verb is a verb that takes a direct object. It is transitive because the action passes over and directly affects something or someone in some way.

Je vois mon ami. / I see my friend. → *Je le vois.* / I see him.
Je ferme la fenêtre. / I am closing the window. → *Je la ferme.* / I'm closing it.

When the direct object of the verb is a pronoun, it is usually placed in front of the verb. The only time it is placed after the verb is in the affirmative imperative. To get an idea of the position of direct object pronouns, see Word Order of Elements in French Sentences, §11.

§7.3–3 Intransitive Verbs

An intransitive verb is a verb that does not take a direct object. Such a verb is called intransitive because the action does not pass over and directly affect anyone or anything.

La maîtresse parle. / The teacher is talking.
Elle est partie tôt. / She left early.
Elles sont descendues vite. / They came down quickly.
Nous sommes montées lentement. / We went up slowly.

An intransitive verb takes an indirect object.

La maîtresse parle aux élèves. / The teacher is talking to the students.

Here the indirect object noun is *élèves* because it is preceded by *aux* / to the.

La maîtresse leur parle. / The teacher is talking to them.

Here the indirect object is the pronoun *leur,* meaning "to them."

§7.4 PRESENT PARTICIPLE

Regular Formation

The present participle is regularly formed in the following way: Take the *nous* form of the present indicative tense of the verb you have in mind, drop the first person plural ending -*ons,* and add -*ant.* That ending is equivalent to -*ing* in English.

Infinitive	Present Tense 1st Person Plural	Drop -ons	add -ant	Present Participle
finir / to finish	nous finissons	finiss	ant	finissant
manger / to eat	nous mangeons	mange	ant	mangeant
vendre / to sell	nous vendons	vend	ant	vendant
faire / to do; make	nous faisons	fais	ant	faisant
dire / to say; tell	nous disons	dis	ant	disant

Common Irregular Present Participles

Infinitive	Present Participle
avoir to have être to be savoir to know	ayant étant sachant

Mnemonic tip | If you're not sure which is a present participle and which is a past participle in French, associate the n in present with the *n* in the French ending -*ant* of a present participle.

En + Present Participle

The present participle in French is used primarily with the preposition *en,* meaning "on," "upon," "in," "while," "by."

en chantant / while singing
en finissant / upon finishing
en vendant / by selling
en mangeant / upon eating, while eating
en voyageant / by traveling
en ayant / on having
en étant / on being, upon being
en sachant / upon knowing

The present participle is sometimes used as an adjective.

un enfant amusant / an amusing child (boy)
une enfant amusante / an amusing child (girl)

§7.5 VERBS AND PREPOSITIONS

Verb + à + Noun or Pronoun

- *assister à quelque chose (à un assemblage, à une réunion, à un spectacle, etc.)* / to attend or be present at (a gathering, a meeting, a theatrical presentation, etc.)

  Allez-vous assister à la conférence du professeur Godard? / Are you going to attend (be present at) Professor Godard's lecture? —*Oui, je vais y assister.* / Yes, I am going to attend it.

- *demander à quelqu'un* / to ask someone

  Demandez à la dame où s'arrête l'autobus. / Ask the lady where the bus stops.

- *désobéir à quelqu'un* / to disobey someone

  Ce chien ne désobéit jamais à son maître. / This dog never disobeys his master.
  Il ne lui désobéit jamais. / He never disobeys him.

- *être à quelqu'un* / to belong to someone

  Ce livre est à Victor. / This book belongs to Victor.

- *faire attention à quelqu'un ou à quelque chose* / to pay attention to someone or to something

  Faites attention au professeur. / Pay attention to the professor.

- *s'intéresser à quelqu'un ou à quelque chose* / to be interested in someone or something

  Je m'intéresse aux sports. / I am interested in sports.

- *jouer à* / to play (a game or sport)

  Il aime bien jouer à la balle. / He likes to play ball.
  Elle aime bien jouer au tennis. / She likes to play tennis.

- *obéir à quelqu'un* / to obey someone

  Une personne honorable obéit à ses parents. / An honorable person obeys his (her) parents.

- *participer à quelque chose* / to participate in something

  Je participe aux sports. / I participate in sports.

- *penser à quelqu'un ou à quelque chose* / to think of (about) someone or something

  Je pense à mes amis. / I am thinking of my friends.
  Je pense à eux. / I am thinking of them.
  Je pense à mon travail. / I am thinking about my work.
  J'y pense. / I am thinking about it.

- *répondre à quelqu'un ou à quelque chose* / to answer someone or something

    J'ai répondu au professeur. / I answered the teacher.
    Je lui ai répondu. / I answered him.
    J'ai répondu à la lettre. / I answered the letter.
    J'y ai répondu. / I answered it.

- *ressembler à quelqu'un* / to resemble someone

    Il ressemble beaucoup à sa mère. / He resembles his mother a lot.

- *réussir à quelque chose* / to succeed in something
    réussir à un examen / to pass an examination

    Il a réussi à l'examen. / He passed the exam.

- *téléphoner à quelqu'un* / to telephone someone

    Marie a téléphoné à Paul. / Marie telephoned Paul.
    Elle lui a téléphoné. / She telephoned him.

Verb + *à* + Infinitive

- *aider à* / to help

    Roger aide son petit frère à faire son devoir de mathématiques.
    Roger is helping his little brother to do his math homework.

- *s'amuser à* / to amuse oneself, enjoy, have fun

    Il y a des élèves qui s'amusent à mettre le professeur en colère. / There are pupils who enjoy making the teacher angry.

- *apprendre à* / to learn

    J'apprends à lire. / I am learning to read.

- *s'attendre à* / to expect

    Je m'attendais à trouver une salle de classe vide. / I was expecting to find an empty classroom.

- *avoir à* / to have to, to be obliged to (do something)

    J'ai mes devoirs à faire ce soir. / I have to do my homework tonight.

- *commencer à* / to begin

    il commence à pleuvoir. / It is beginning to rain.

- *continuer à* / to continue

    Je continue à étudier le français. / I am continuing to study French.

- *décider quelqu'un à* / to persuade someone

    J'ai décidé mon père à me prêter quelques francs. / I persuaded my father to lend me a few francs.

- *se décider à* / to make up one's mind

    Il s'est décidé à l'épouser. / He made up his mind to marry her.

- *demander à* / to ask, request

    Elle demande à parler. / She asks to speak.

- *encourager à* / to encourage

    Je l'ai encouragé à suivre un cours de français. / I encouraged him to take a course in French.

- *enseigner à* / to teach

    Je vous enseigne à lire en français. / I am teaching you to read in French.

- *s'habituer à* / to get used (to)

    Je m'habitue à parler français couramment. / I am getting used to speaking French fluently.

- *hésiter à* / to hesitate

    J'hésite à répondre à sa lettre. / I hesitate to reply to her (his) letter.

- *inviter à* / to invite

    Monsieur et Madame Boivin ont invité les Béry à dîner chez eux. / Mr. and Mrs. Boivin invited the Bérys to have dinner at their house.

- *se mettre à* / to begin

    L'enfant se met à rire. / The child is beginning to laugh.

- *parvenir à* / to succeed

    Elle est parvenue à être docteur. / She succeeded in becoming a doctor.

- *se plaire à* / to take pleasure in

    Il se plaît à taquiner ses amis. / He takes pleasure in teasing his friends.

- *recommencer à* / to begin again

    Il recommence à pleuvoir. / It is beginning to rain again.

- *avoir peur de* / to be afraid of

    Le petit garçon a peur de traverser la rue seul. / The little boy is afraid of crossing the street alone.

- *cesser de* / to stop, cease

    Il a cessé de pleuvoir. / It has stopped raining.

- *craindre de* / to be afraid of, fear

    La petite fille craint de traverser la rue seule. / The little girl is afraid of crossing the street alone.

- *décider de* / to decide

    J'ai décidé de partir tout de suite. / I decided to leave immediately.

- *demander de* / to ask, request

    Je vous demande de parler. / I am asking you to speak.

    [Note that here the subjects are different: *I* am asking *you* to speak; but when the subjects are the same, use *demander à: Elle demande à parler.* / She is asking to speak.]

- *se dépêcher de* / to hurry

    Je me suis dépêché de venir chez vous pour vous dire quelque chose. / I hurried to come to your place in order to tell you something.

- *empêcher de* / to keep from, prevent

    Je vous empêche de sortir. / I prevent you from going out.

- *essayer de* / to try

    J'essaye d'ouvrir la porte mais je ne peux pas. / I'm trying to open the door but I can't.

- *féliciter de* / to congratulate

    On m'a félicité d'avoir gagné le prix. / I was congratulated on having won the prize.

- *finir de* / to finish

    J'ai fini de travailler sur cette composition. / I have finished working on this composition.

- *se hâter de* / to hurry

    Je me hâte de venir chez toi. / I am hurrying to come to your house.

- *offrir de* / to offer

    J'ai offert d'écrire une lettre pour elle. / I offered to write a
    letter for her.

- *oublier de* / to forget

    J'ai oublié de vous donner la monnaie. / I forgot to give you the
    change.

- *persuader de* / to persuade

    J'ai persuadé mon père de me prêter quelques francs. / I
    persuaded my father to lend me a few francs.

- *prendre garde de* / to take care not to

    Prenez garde de tomber. / Be careful not to fall.

- *prier de* / to beg

    Je vous prie d'arrêter. / I beg you to stop.

- *promettre de* / to promise

    J'ai promis de venir chez toi à huit heures. / I promised to come
    to your place at eight o'clock.

- *refuser de* / to refuse

    Je refuse de le croire. / I refuse to believe it.

- *regretter de* / to regret, be sorry

    Je regrette d'être obligé de vous dire cela. / I am sorry to be
    obliged to tell you that.

- *remercier de* / to thank

    Je vous remercie d'être venu si vite. / I thank you for coming
    (having come) so quickly. (Use *remercier de* + infinitive or +
    abstract noun. Use *remercier pour* + concrete object.)

- *se souvenir de* / to remember

    Tu vois? Je me suis souvenu de venir chez toi. / You see? I
    remembered to come to your house.

- *tâcher de* / to try

    Tâche de finir tes devoirs avant de sortir. / Try to finish your
    homework before going out.

- *venir de* / to have just (done something)

    Je viens de manger. / I have just eaten. (I just ate.)

Verb + *à* + Noun + *de* + Infinitive

The model to follow is: *J'ai conseillé à Robert de suivre un cours de français.* / I advised Robert to take a course in French.

- *conseiller à* / to advise

  J'ai conseillé à Jeanne de se marier. / I advised Joan to get married.

- *défendre à* / to forbid

  Mon père défend à mon frère de fumer. / My father forbids my brother to smoke.

- *demander à* / to ask, request

  J'ai demandé à Marie de venir. / I asked Mary to come.

- *dire à* / to say, to tell

  J'ai dit à Charles de venir. / I told Charles to come.

- *interdire à* / to forbid

  Mon père interdit à mon frère de fumer. / My father forbids my brother to smoke.

- *permettre à* / to permit

  J'ai permis à l'étudiant de partir quelques minutes avant la fin de la classe. / I permitted the student to leave a few minutes before the end of class.

- *promettre à* / to promise

  J'ai promis à mon ami d'arriver à l'heure. / I promised my friend to arrive on time.

- *téléphoner à* / to telephone

  J'ai téléphoné à Marcel de venir me voir. / I phoned Marcel to come to see me.

Verb + Other Prepositions

- *commencer par* + infinitive / to begin by + present participle

  La présidente a commencé par discuter des problèmes de la société. / The president began by discussing problems in society.

- *s'entendre avec quelqu'un* / to get along with someone

  Jean s'entend avec Christophe. / John gets along with Christopher.

- *entrer dans* + noun / to enter, go in

  Elle est entrée dans le restaurant. / **She went into the restaurant.**

- *insister pour* + infinitive / to insist on, upon

  J'insiste pour obtenir tous mes droits. / **I insist on obtaining all my rights.**

- *se marier avec quelqu'un* / to marry someone

  Elle va se marier avec lui. / **She is going to marry him.**

- *se mettre en colère* / to become angry, upset

  Monsieur Leduc se met en colère facilement. / **Mr. Leduc gets angry easily.**

- *se mettre en route* / to start out, set out

  Ils se sont mis en route dès l'aube. / **They started out at dawn.**

- *remercier pour* + a concrete noun / to thank for

  Je vous remercie pour le joli cadeau. / **I thank you for the pretty present. (Remember to use** *remercier de* **+ an abstract noun or + infinitive:** *Je vous remercie de votre bonté.* **/ I thank you for your kindness.** *Je vous remercie d'être venue si vite.* **/ I thank you for coming so quickly.)**

Verb + no preposition + Infinitive

The following verbs take *no* preposition and are followed directly by the infinitive.

- *adorer* / to adore, love

  Madame Morin adore mettre tous ses bijoux avant de sortir. / **Mrs. Morin loves to put on all her jewelry before going out.**

- *aimer* / to like

  J'aime lire. / **I like to read.**

- *aimer mieux* / to prefer

  J'aime mieux rester ici. / **I prefer to stay here.**

- *aller* / to go

  Je vais faire mes devoirs. / **I am going to do my homework.**

- *compter* / to intend

  Je compte aller en France l'été prochain. / **I intend to go to France next summer.**

- *croire* / to believe

  Il croit être innocent. / He believes he is innocent.

- *désirer* / to desire, wish

  Je désire prendre une tasse de café. / I wish to have a cup of coffee.

- *devoir* / to have to, ought to

  Je dois faire mes devoirs avant de sortir. / I have to do my homework before going out.

- *écouter* / to listen to

  J'écoute chanter les enfants. / I am listening to the children singing.

- *entendre* / to hear

  J'entends chanter les enfants. / I hear the children singing.

- *espérer* / to hope

  J'espère aller en France. / I hope to go to France.

- *faire* / to cause; to make; to have something done by someone

  Le professeur fait travailler les élèves dans la salle de classe. / The teacher has the pupils work in the classroom.

- *falloir* / to be necessary

  Il faut être honnête. / One must be honest.

- *laisser* / to let, allow

  Je vous laisse partir. / I am letting you go.

- *paraître* / to appear, seem

  Elle paraît être capable. / She appears to be capable.

- *penser* / to think, plan, intend

  Je pense aller à Paris. / I intend to go to Paris.

- *pouvoir* / to be able, can

  Je peux marcher mieux maintenant. / I can walk better now.

- *préférer* / to prefer

  Je préfère manger maintenant. / I prefer to eat now.

- *regarder* / to look at

  Je regarde voler les oiseaux. / I am looking at the birds flying.

- *savoir* / to know, know how

    Je sais nager. / I know how to swim.

- *valoir mieux* / to be better

    Il vaut mieux être honnête. / It is better to be honest.

- *vouloir* / to want

    Je veux venir chez vous. / I want to come to your house.

Verbs That Do Not Require a Preposition

- *attendre* / to wait for

    J'attends l'autobus depuis vingt minutes. / I have been waiting for the bus for twenty minutes.

- *chercher* / to look for

    Je cherche mon livre. / I'm looking for my book.

- *demander* / to ask for

    Je demande une réponse. / I am asking for a reply.

- *écouter* / to listen to

    J'écoute la musique. / I am listening to the music.
    J'écoute le professeur. / I am listening to the teacher.

- *envoyer chercher* / to send for

    J'ai envoyé chercher le docteur. / I sent for the doctor.

- *essayer* / to try on

    Elle a essayé une jolie robe. / She tried on a pretty dress.

- *mettre* / to put on

    Elle a mis la robe rouge. / She put on the red dress.

- *payer* / to pay for

    J'ai payé le dîner. / I paid for the dinner.

- *pleurer* / to cry about, cry over

    Elle pleure la perte de son petit chien. / She is crying over the loss of her little dog.

- *regarder* / to look at

    Je regarde le ciel. / I am looking at the sky.

§7.6 COMPLETE CONJUGATION OF AN *AVOIR* VERB

Present participle: *parlant* / talking, speaking; Past participle: *parlé* / talked, spoken; Infinitive *parler* / to talk, to speak

Present indicative

je parle, tu parles, il (elle, on) parle; nous parlons, vous parlez, ils (elles) parlent

I talk, you talk, he (she, it, one) talks; we talk, you talk, they talk
OR
I do talk, etc.
OR
I am talking, etc.

Imperfect indicative

je parlais, tu parlais, il (elle, on) parlait; nous parlions, vous parliez, ils (elles) parlaient

I was talking, you were talking, he (she, it, one) was talking; we were talking, you were talking, they were talking
OR
I used to talk, etc.
OR
I talked, etc.

Past definite

je parlai, tu parlas, il (elle, on) parla; nous parlâmes, vous parlâtes, ils (elles) parlèrent

I talked, you talked, he (she, it, one) talked; we talked, you talked, they talked
OR
I did talk, etc.

Future

je parlerai, tu parleras, il (elle, on) parlera; nous parlerons, vous parlerez, ils (elles) parleront

I shall talk, you will talk, he (she, it, one) will talk; we shall talk, you will talk, they will talk

Conditional present

je parlerais, tu parlerais, il (elle, on) parlerait; nous parlerions, vous parleriez, ils (elles) parleraient

I would talk, you would talk, he (she, it, one) would talk; we would talk, you would talk, they would talk

Present subjunctive	*que je parle, que tu parles, qu'il (qu'elle, qu'on) parle; que nous parlions, que vous parliez, qu'ils (qu'elles) parlent*
	that I may talk, that you may talk, that he (she, it, one) may talk; that we may talk, that you may talk, that they may talk

Imperfect subjunctive	*que je parlasse, que tu parlasses, qu'il (qu'elle, qu'on) parlât; que nous parlassions, que vous parlassiez, qu'ils (qu'elles) parlassent*
	that I might talk, that you might talk, that he (she, it, one) might talk; that we might talk, that you might talk, that they might talk

Past indefinite	*j'ai parlé, tu as parlé, il (elle, on) a parlé; nous avons parlé, vous avez parlé, ils (elles) ont parlé*
	I talked, you talked, he (she, it, one) talked; we talked, you talked, they talked
	OR
	I have talked, you have talked, he (she, it, one) has talked; we have talked, you have talked, they have talked
	OR
	I did talk, you did talk, he (she, it, one) did talk; we did talk, you did talk, they did talk

Pluperfect indicative	*j'avais parlé, tu avais parlé, il (elle, on) avait parlé; nous avions parlé, vous aviez parlé, ils (elles) avaient parlé*
	I had talked, you had talked, he (she, it, one) had talked; we had talked, you had talked, they had talked

Past anterior	*j'eus parlé, tu eus parlé, il (elle, on) eut parlé; nous eûmes parlé, vous eûtes parlé, ils (elles) eurent parlé*
	I had talked, you had talked, he (she, it, one) had talked; we had talked, you had talked, they had talked

Future perfect	*j'aurai parlé, tu auras parlé, il (elle, on) aura parlé; nous aurons parlé, vous aurez parlé, ils (elles) auront parlé*
	I shall have talked, you will have talked, he (she, it, one) will have talked; we shall have talked, you will have talked, they will have talked
Conditional perfect	*j'aurais parlé, tu aurais parlé, il (elle, on) aurait parlé; nous aurions parlé, vous auriez parlé, ils (elles) auraient parlé*
	I would have talked, you would have talked, he (she, it, one) would have talked; we would have talked, you would have talked, they would have talked
Past subjunctive	*que j'aie parlé, que tu aies parlé, qu'il (qu'elle, qu'on) ait parlé; que nous ayons parlé, que vous ayez parlé, qu'ils (qu'elles) aient parlé*
	that I may have talked, that you may have talked, that he (she, it, one) may have talked; that we may have talked, that you may have talked, that they may have talked
Pluperfect subjunctive	*que j'eusse parlé, que tu eusses parlé, qu'il (qu'elle, qu'on) eût parlé; que nous eussions parlé, que vous eussiez parlé, qu'ils (qu'elles) eussent parlé*
	that I might have talked, that you might have talked, that he (she, it, one) might have talked; that we might have talked, that you might have talked, that they might have talked
Imperative	*parle, parlons, parlez*
	talk, let's talk, talk

§7.7 COMPLETE CONJUGA-TION OF AN *ÊTRE* VERB

Present participle: *venant* / coming; Past participle; *venu* / come; Infinitive: *venir* / to come

Present indicative	*je viens, tu viens, il (elle, on) vient; nous venons, vous venez, ils (elles) viennent*

I come, you come, he (she, it, one) comes; we come, you come, they come

OR

I do come, etc.

OR

I am coming, etc.

Imperfect indicative	*je venais, tu venais, il (elle, on) venait; nous venions, vous veniez, ils (elles) venaient*

I was coming, you were coming, he (she, it, one) was coming; we were coming, you were coming, they were coming

OR

I used to come, etc.

OR

I came, etc.

Past definite	*je vins, tu vins, il (elle, on) vint; nous vînmes, vous vîntes, ils (elles) vinrent*

I came, you came, he (she, it, one) came; we came, you came, they came

OR

I did come, etc.

Future	*je viendrai, tu viendras, il (elle, on) viendra; nous viendrons, vous viendrez, ils (elles) viendront*

I shall come, you will come, he (she, it, one) will come; we shall come, you will come, they will come

Conditional present	*je viendrais, tu viendrais, il (elle, on) viendrait; nous viendrions, vous viendriez, ils (elles) viendraient*

I would come, you would come, he (she, it, one) would come; we would come, you would come, they would come

Present subjunctive	*que je vienne, que tu viennes, qu'il (qu'elle, qu'on) vienne; que nous venions, que vous veniez, qu'ils (qu'elles) viennent*
	that I may come, that you may come, that he (she, it, one) may come; that we may come, that you may come, that they may come
Imperfect subjunctive	*que je vinsse, que tu vinsses, qu'il (qu'elle, qu'on) vînt; que nous vinssions, que vous vinssiez, qu'ils (qu'elles) vinssent*
	that I might come, that you might come, that he (she, it, one) might come; that we might come, that you might come; that they might come
Past indefinite	*je suis venu(e), tu es venu(e), il (on) est venu, elle est venue; nous sommes venu(e)s, vous êtes venu(e)(s), ils sont venus, elles sont venues*
	I came, you came, he (she, it, one) came; we came, you came, they came
	OR
	I have come, etc.
	OR
	I did come, etc.
Pluperfect indicative	*j'étais venu(e), tu étais venu(e), il, on était venu, elle était venue; nous étions venu(e)s, vous étiez venu(e)(s), ils étaient venus, elles étaient venues*
	I had come, you had come, he (she, it, one) had come; we had come, you had come, they had come
Past anterior	*je fus venu(e), tu fus venu(e), il (on) fut venu, elle fut venue; nous fûmes venu(e)s, vous fûtes venu(e)(s), ils furent venus, elles furent venues*
	I had come, you had come, he (she, it, one) had come; we had come, you had come, they had come

Future perfect	*je serai venu(e), tu seras venu(e), il (on) sera venu, elle sera venue; nous serons venu(e)s, vous serez venu(e)(s), ils seront venus, elles seront venues*
	I shall have come, you will have come, he (she, it, one) will have come; we shall have come, you will have come, they will have come
Conditional perfect	*je serais venu(e), tu serais venu(e), il (on) serait venu, elle serait venue; nous serions venu(e)s, vous seriez venu(e)(s), ils seraient venus, elles seraient venues*
	I would have come, you would have come, he (she, it, one) would have come; we would have come, you would have come, they would have come
Past subjunctive	*que je sois venu(e), que tu sois venu(e), qu'il (on) soit venu, qu'elle soit venue; que nous soyons venu(e)s, que vous soyez venu(e)(s), qu'ils soient venus, qu'elles soient venues*
	that I may have come, that you may have come, that he (she, it, one) may have come; that we may have come, that you may have come, that they may have come
Pluperfect subjunctive	*que je fusse venu(e), que tu fusses venu(e), qu'il (qu'on) fût venu, qu'elle fût venue; que nous fussions venu(e)s, que vous fussiez venu(e)(s), qu'ils fussent venus, qu'elles fussent venues*
	that I might have come, that you might have come, that he (she, it, one) might have come; that we might have come, that you might have come, that they might have come
Imperative	*viens, venons, venez*
	come, let's come, come

§7.8
TENSES AND
MOODS
§7.8–1
Present
Indicative
Tense

The *present indicative* is the most frequently used tense in French and English. It indicates:

- An action or a state of being at the present time.

    Je vais à l'école maintenant. / I am going to school now.
    Je pense; donc, je suis. / I think; therefore, I am.

- Habitual action.

    Je vais à la bibliothèque tous les jours. / I go to the library every day.

- A general truth, something that is permanently true.

    Deux et deux font quatre. / Two and two are four.
    Voir c'est croire. / Seeing is believing.

- Vividness when talking or writing about past events.

    Marie-Antoinette est condamnée à mort. Elle monte dans la charrette qui est en route pour la guillotine. / Marie-Antoinette is condemned to die. She gets into the cart and is on her way to the guillotine.

- A near future.

    Il arrive demain. / He arrives tomorrow.

- An action or state of being that occurred in the past and continues up to the present. In English, this tense is the present perfect, which is formed with the present tense of "to have" plus the past participle of the verb you are using.

    Je suis ici depuis dix minutes. / I have been here for ten minutes. (I am still here at present.)

This tense is regularly formed as follows:

- Drop the *-er* ending of an infinitive like *parler,* and add *-e, -es, -e; -ons, -ez, -ent.*

    You then get:
    je parle, tu parles, il (elle, on) parle; nous parlons, vous parlez, ils (elles) parlent

- Drop the *-ir* ending of an infinitive like *finir,* and add *-is, -is, -it; -issons, -issez, -issent.*

  You then get:
  je finis, tu finis, il (elle, on) finit; nous finissons, vous finissez, ils (ells) finissent

- Drop the *-re* ending of an infinitive like *vendre,* and add *-s, -s, —; -ons, -ez, -ent.*

  You then get:
  je vends, tu vends, il (elle, on) vend; nous vendons, vous vendez, ils (elles) vendent

  For the present tense of *avoir* and *être,* see §7.18.

§7.8–2 Imperfect Indicative Tense

The *imperfect indicative* is a past tense. It is used to indicate:

- An action that was going on in the past at the same time as another action.

  Il lisait pendant que j'écrivais. / He was reading while I was writing.

- An action that was going on in the past when another action occurred.

  Il lisait quand je suis entré. / He was reading when I came in.

- An action that was performed habitually in the past.

  Nous allions à la plage tous les jours. / We used to go to the beach every day.

- A description of a mental or physical condition in the past.

  (mental) *Il était triste quand je l'ai vu.* / He was sad when I saw him.
  (physical) *Quand ma mère était jeune, elle était belle.* / When my mother was young, she was beautiful.

- An action or state of being that occurred in the past and lasted for a certain length of time prior to another past action.

  J'attendais l'autobus depuis dix minutes quand il est arrivé. / I had been waiting for the bus for ten minutes when it arrived.

This tense is regularly formed as follows:
  For *-er, -ir,* and *-re* verbs, take the *"nous"* form in the present indicative tense of the verb you have in mind, drop the first person plural ending *(-ons),* and add the endings *-ais, -ais, -ait; -ions, -iez, -aient.*

Mnemonic tip | The vowel *i* is in each of the six endings and *i* is the first letter of the *imperfect* tense.

For the imperfect indicative of *avoir* and *être*, see §7.18.

§7.8–3
Past Simple Tense

This past tense expresses an action that took place at some definite time. It is not ordinarily used in conversational French or in informal writing. It is a literary tense — used in formal writing, such as history and literature.

The past simple tense is regularly formed as follows:
For all *-er* verbs, drop the *-er* of the infinitive and add *-ai, -as, -a; -âmes, -âtes, -èrent.*
For regular *-ir* and *-re* verbs, drop the ending of the infinitive and add the endings *-is, -is, -it; -îmes, -îtes, -irent.*

Il alla en Afrique. / He went to Africa.
Il voyagea en Amérique. / He traveled to America.
Elle fut heureuse. / She was happy.
Elle eut un grand bonheur. / She had great happiness.

For the past definite of *avoir* and *être*, see §7.18.

§7.8–4
Future Tense

In French and English the *future* tense is used to express an action or a state of being which will take place at some time in the future.

J'irai en France l'été prochain. / I will go to France next summer.
J'y penserai. / I will think about it.
Je partirai dès qu'il arrivera. / I will leave as soon as he arrives.
Je te dirai tout quand tu seras ici. / I will tell you all when you are here.

If the action of the verb you are using is not past or present and if future time is implied, the future tense is used when the clause begins with the following conjunctions: *aussitôt que* / as soon as, *dès que* / as soon as, *quand* / when, *lorsque* / when, and *tant que* / as long as.

This tense is regularly formed as follows:
Add the following endings to the whole infinitive: *-ai, -as, -a, -ons, -ez, -ont.* For *-re* verbs you must drop the *e* in *-re* before you add the future endings.

For the future of *avoir* and *être*, see §7.18.

§7.8-5
Conditional
Present Tense

The conditional mood is used in French and English to express:

- An action that you would do if something else were possible.

    Je ferais le travail si j'en avais le temps. / I would do the work if I had the time.

- A conditional desire.

    J'aimerais du thé. / I would like some tea.
    Je voudrais du café. / I would like some coffee.

- An obligation or duty.

    Je devrais étudier pour l'examen. / I should study for the examination.

The conditional has two tenses, the present and the past.

The present conditional is regularly formed as follows:
Add the following endings to the whole infinitive: *-ais, -ais, -ait; -ions, -iez, -aient.* For *-re* verbs you must drop the *e* in *-re* before you add the conditional endings. Note that these endings are the same ones you use to form regularly the imperfect indicative. For the conditional of *avoir* and *être*, see §7.18.

§7.8-6
Present
Subjunctive
Tense

The subjunctive mood is used in French much more than in English. It is used in the following ways:

- After a verb that expresses some kind of insistence, preference, or suggestion.

    Nous insistons que vous soyez ici à l'heure. / We insist that you be here on time.
    Je préfère qu'il fasse le travail maintenant. / I prefer that he do the work now.
    Le juge exige qu'il soit puni. / The judge demands that he be punished.

- After a verb that expresses doubt, fear, joy, sorrow, or some other emotion.

    Sylvie doute qu'il vienne. / Sylvia doubts that he is coming.
    Je suis heureux qu'il vienne. / I'm happy that he is coming.
    Je regrette qu'il soit malade. / I'm sorry that he is sick.

- After certain conjunctions.

  Elle partira à moins qu'il ne vienne. / She will leave unless he
  comes.
  Je resterai jusqu'à ce qu'il vienne. / I will stay until he comes.
  Quoiqu'elle soit belle, il ne l'aime pas. / Although she is
  beautiful, he does not love her.
  Le professeur l'explique pour qu'elle comprenne. / The teacher
  is explaining it so that she may understand.

- After certain impersonal expressions that show a need, a
  doubt, a possibility or an impossibility.

  Il est urgent qu'il vienne. / It is urgent that he come.
  Il vaut mieux qu'il vienne. / It is better that he come.
  Il est possible qu'il vienne. / It is possible that he will come.
  Il est douteux qu'il vienne. / It is doubtful that he will come.

The present subjunctive is regularly formed by dropping
the *-ant* ending of the present participle of the verb you are
using and adding the endings *-e, -es, -e; -ions, -iez, -ent.*

For the present subjunctive of *avoir* and *être*, see §7.18.
See also Subjunctive, §7.15.

§7.8–7 Imperfect Subjunctive Tense

The *imperfect subjunctive* is used in the same ways as the
present subjunctive, that is, after certain verbs, conjunctions, and impersonal expressions. The main difference
between these two is the time of the action. If present, use
the present subjunctive. If the action is related to the past,
the imperfect subjunctive is used, provided that the action
was not completed.

Je voulais qu'il vînt. / I wanted him to come. (action not
completed; he did not come while I
wanted him to come)

Note: The subjunctive of *venir* is used because *vouloir*
requires the subjunctive *after* it. In conversational French
and informal writing, the imperfect subjunctive is
avoided. Use, instead, the present subjunctive.

Je voulais qu'il vienne. / I wanted him to come.
Je le lui expliquais pour qu'elle le comprît. / I was explaining it
to her so that she might understand it. (action not completed;
the understanding was not completed at the time of the
explaining)

Note: The subjunctive of *comprendre* is used because the conjunction *pour que* requires the subjunctive *after* it. Again, avoid using the imperfect subjunctive in conversation and informal writing. Use, instead, the present subjunctive: *Je le lui expliquais pour qu'elle le comprenne.*

The imperfect subjunctive is regularly formed by dropping the endings of the *passé simple* of the verb you are using and adding the following endings:

> *-er* verbs: *-asse, -asses, -ât; -assions, -assiez, -assent*
> *-ir* verbs: *-isse, -isses, -ît; -issions, -issiez, -issent*
> *-re* verbs: *-usse, -usses, -ût; -ussions, -ussiez, -ussent*

For the imperfect subjunctive of *avoir* and *être,* see §7.18. See also Subjunctive, §7.15.

§7.8–8 Past Indefinite Tense

This past tense expresses an action that took place at no definite time. It is used in conversational French, correspondence, and other informal writing. The past indefinite is used more and more in literature these days and is taking the place of the past definite. It is a compound tense because it is formed with the present indicative of *avoir* or *être* (depending on which of these two auxiliaries is required to form a compound tense) plus the past participle. See §7.3 for the distinction made between verbs conjugated with *avoir* or *être.* This is the **passé composé.**

> *Il est allé à l'école.* / He went to school; He did go to school; He has gone to school.
> *J'ai mangé dans ce restaurant de nombreuses fois.* / I have eaten in this restaurant many times.
> *J'ai parlé au garçon.* / I spoke to the boy; I have spoken to the boy; I did speak to the boy.

§7.8–9 Pluperfect Tense

In French and English this tense (also called the *past perfect*) is used to express an action that happened in the past before another past action. Since it is used in relation to another past action, the other past action is expressed in either the past indefinite or the imperfect indicative in French. The pluperfect is used in formal writing and literature as well as in conversational French and informal writing. It is a compound tense because it is formed with the imperfect indicative of *avoir* or *être* (depending on which of these two auxiliaries is required to form a compound tense) plus the past participle. See §7.3 for the distinction made between verbs conjugated with *avoir* or *être*.

Je me suis rappelé que j'avais oublié de le lui dire. / I remembered that I had forgotten to tell him.

Note: It would be incorrect to say: I remembered that I forgot to tell him. The point here is that first I forgot; then I remembered. Both actions are in the past. The action that occurred in the past *before* the other past action is in the pluperfect. And in this example it is "I had forgotten" (*j'avais oublié*).

J'avais étudié la leçon que le professeur a expliquée. / I had studied the lesson that the teacher explained.

Note: First I studied the lesson; then the teacher explained it. Both actions are in the past. The action that occurred in the past before the other past action is in the pluperfect. And in this example it is "I had studied" (*j'avais étudié*).

J'étais fatigué ce matin parce que je n'avais pas dormi. / I was tired this morning because I had not slept.

§7.8 – 10 Past Anterior Tense

This tense is similar to the pluperfect indicative. The main difference is that in French it is a literary tense; that is, it is used in formal writing such as history and literature. More and more French writers today use the pluperfect indicative instead of the past anterior. The past anterior is a compound tense and is formed with the *passé simple* of *avoir* or *être* (depending on which of these two auxiliaries is required to form a compound tense) plus the past participle. It is ordinarily introduced by conjunctions of time: *après que, aussitôt que, dès que, lorsque, quand.*

Quand il eut tout mangé, il partit. / When he had eaten everything, he left.

§7.8 – 11 Future Perfect Tense

In French and English this tense (also called the *future anterior*) is used to express an action that will happen in the future *before* another future action. Since it is used in relation to another future action, the other future action is expressed in the simple future in French. It is used in conversation and informal writing as well as in formal writing and in literature. It is a compound tense because it is formed with the future of *avoir* or *être* (depending on which of these two auxiliaries is required to form a compound tense) plus the past participle of the verb you are using. In English, it is formed by using "will have" plus the past participle of the verb you are using.

Elle arrivera demain et j'aurai fini le travail. / She will arrive tomorrow and I will have finished the work.

Note: First I will finish the work; then she will arrive. The action that will occur in the future *before* the other future action is in the future anterior.

Quand elle arrivera demain, j'aurai fini le travail. / When she arrives tomorrow, I will have finished the work.

Note: The idea of future time here is the same as in the preceding example. In English, the present tense is used ("When she arrives . . .") to express a near future. In French, the future is used *(Quand elle arrivera . . .)* because *quand* precedes and the action will take place in the future.

§7.8 – 12 Conditional Perfect Tense

This is used in French and English to express an action that you would have done if something else had been possible; that is, you would have done something on condition that something else had been possible. It is a compound tense because it is formed with the conditional of *avoir* or *être* plus the past participle of the verb you are using. In English, it is formed by using "would have" plus the past participle.

J'aurais fait le travail si j'avais étudié. / I would have done the work if I had studied.
J'aurais fait le travail si j'en avais eu le temps. / I would have done the work if I had had the time.

§7.8 – 13 Past Subjunctive Tense

This tense is used to express an action that took place in the past in relation to the present. It is like the past indefinite, except that the auxiliary verb (*avoir* or *être*) is in the present subjunctive. The subjunctive is used because what precedes is a certain verb, conjunction, or impersonal expression. The past subjunctive is also used in relation to a future time when another action will be completed. In French this tense is used in formal writing and in literature as well as in conversation and informal writing. It is a compound tense because it is formed with the present subjunctive of *avoir* or *être* as the auxiliary plus the past participle of the verb you are using.

A past action in relation to the present:
Il est possible qu'elle soit partie. / It is possible that she has left.
Je doute qu'il ait fait cela. / I doubt that he did that.

An action that will take place in the future:
Je désire que vous soyez rentré avant dix heures. / I want you to be back before ten o'clock.

§7.8 – 14
Pluperfect
Subjunctive
Tense

This tense (also called the *past perfect*) is used for the same reasons as the imperfect subjunctive — that is, after certain verbs, conjunctions, and impersonal expressions. The main difference between the imperfect and the pluperfect subjunctive is the time of the action in the past. If the action was not completed, the imperfect subjunctive is used; if the action was completed, the pluperfect is used. In French, it is used only in formal writing and literature.

Il était possible qu'elle fût partie. / It was possible that she might have left.

NOTE: Avoid this tense in French. Use the past subjunctive instead: *Il était possible qu'elle soit partie.*

§7.8 – 15
Imperative
Mood

The *imperative* mood is used in French and English to express a command or request. It is also used to express an indirect request made in the third person. In both languages it is formed by dropping the subject and using the present tense. There are a few exceptions in both languages when the present subjunctive is used.

Sortez! / Get out!   *Asseyez-vous!* / Sit down!
Entrez! / Come in!   *Levez-vous!* / Get up!
Soyez à l'heure! / Be on time! (subjunctive used)
Dieu le veuille! / May God grant it! (subjunctive used)
Qu'ils mangent du gâteau! / Let them eat cake! (subjunctive used)

You must drop the final *s* in the second person singular of an *-er* verb. This is done in the affirmative and negative, as in: *Mange!* / Eat! *Ne mange pas!* / Don't eat! However, when the pronouns *y* and *en* are linked to it, the *s* is retained in all regular *-er* verbs and in the verb *aller*. The reason for this is that it makes it easier to link the two elements by pronouncing the *s* as a *z*.

Donnes-en! / Give some!
Manges-en! / Eat some!
Vas-y! / Go there!

§7.9 PASSIVE VOICE

When verbs are used in the active voice, which is almost all the time, the subject performs the action. When the *passive* voice is used, the subject of the sentence is not the performer; the action falls on the subject. The agent (the performer) is sometimes expressed, sometimes not, as is done in English. The passive voice, therefore, is composed of the verb in the passive, which is any tense of *être* + the past participle of the verb you are using to indicate the action performed upon the subject. Since *être* is the verb used in the passive voice, the past participle of your other verb must agree with the subject in gender and number.

Jacqueline a été reçue à l'université. / Jacqueline has been accepted at the university.
Ce livre est écrit par un auteur célèbre. / This book is written by a famous author.
Cette composition a été écrite par un jeune élève. / This composition was written by a young student.

There are certain rules you must remember about the passive voice:

• Usually the preposition *de* is used instead of *par* with such verbs as *aimer, admirer, accompagner, apprécier, voir.*

Jacqueline est aimée de tout le monde. / Jacqueline is liked (loved) by everyone.
BUT
Nous avons été suivis par un chien perdu. / We were followed by a lost dog.

• Avoid the passive voice if the thought can be expressed in the active voice with the indefinite pronoun *on* as the subject.

On vend de bonnes choses dans ce magasin. / Good things are sold in this store.
On parle français ici. / French is spoken here.

- You must avoid using the passive voice with a reflexive verb. Always use a reflexive verb with an active subject.

  Elle s'appelle Jeanne./ She is called Joan.
  Comment se prononce ce mot?/ How is this word pronounced?

§7.10
SI CLAUSE:
A SUMMARY

When the Verb in the *SI* clause is in the:	The Verb in the Main or Result Clause is:
present indicative	present indicative, future, or imperative
imperfect indicative	conditional
pluperfect indicative	conditional perfect

- By *si* we mean "if." Sometimes *si* can mean "whether" and in that case, this summary does not apply because there are no restrictions about the tenses. The sequence of tenses with a *si-* clause is the same in English with an "if" clause.

  Si elle arrive, je pars./ If she arrives, I'm leaving.
  Si elle arrive, je partirai./ If she arrives, I will leave.
  Si elle arrive, partez!/ If she arrives, leave!
  Si Paul étudiait, il aurait de meilleures notes./ If Paul studied, he would have better grades.
  Si Georges avait étudié, il aurait eu de bonnes notes./ If George had studied, he would have had good grades.

§7.11
SPECIAL
USES OF
COMMON
VERBS

DEVOIR/ TO OWE; OUGHT TO

- Present

  Je dois étudier./ I have to study; I must study; I am supposed to study.
  Il doit être fou!/ He must be crazy! He's probably crazy!
  Mon père doit avoir cinquante ans./ My father must be 50 years old.

- Imperfect

  Je devais étudier./ I had to study; I was supposed to study.
  Quand j'étais à l'école, je devais toujours étudier./ When I was in school, I always had to study.
  Ma mère devait avoir cinquante ans quand elle est morte./ My mother was probably 50 years old when she died.

- Future

  Je devrai étudier. / I will have to study.
  Nous devrons faire le travail ce soir. / We will have to do the work this evening.

- Conditional

  Je devrais étudier. / I ought to study. / I should study.
  Vous devriez étudier davantage. / You ought to study more; You should study more.

- Past indefinite

  Je ne suis pas allé(e) au cinéma parce que j'ai dû étudier. / I did not go to the movies because I had to study.
  J'ai dû prendre l'autobus parce qu'il n'y avait pas de train à cette heure-là. / I had to take the bus because there was no train at that hour.
  Robert n'est pas ici. / Robert is not here.
  Il a dû partir. / He must have left; He has probably left; He had to leave.

- Conditional perfect

  J'aurais dû étudier! / I should have studied!
  Vous auriez dû me dire la vérité. / You should have told me the truth.

- With a direct or an indirect object there is still another meaning.

  Je dois de l'argent. / I owe some money.
  Je le lui dois. / I owe it to him (to her).

POUVOIR / TO BE ABLE TO, CAN

- Present

  Je ne peux pas sortir aujourd'hui parce que je suis malade. / I cannot (am unable to) go out today because I am sick.
  Est-ce que je peux entrer? Puis-je entrer? / May I come in?
  Madame Marin peut être malade. / Mrs. Marin may be sick.

  This use of *pouvoir* suggests possibility.

  Je n'en peux plus. / I can't go on any longer.

  This use suggests physical exhaustion.

Il se peut. / It is possible.

This use as a reflexive verb suggests possibility.

Cela ne se peut pas. / That can't be done.

This use as a reflexive verb suggests impossibility.

- Conditional

    Pourriez-vous me prêter dix francs? / Could you lend me ten
        francs?

- Conditional perfect

    Auriez-vous pu venir chez moi? / Could you have come to my
        place?
    Ils auraient pu rater le train. / They might have missed the train.

VOULOIR / TO WANT

- Present

    Je veux aller en France. / I want to go to France.
    Je veux bien sortir avec vous ce soir. / I am willing to go out
        with you this evening.
    Voulez-vous bien vous asseoir? / Would you be good enough to
        sit down?
    Que veut dire ce mot? / What does this word mean?
    Que voulez-vous dire? / What do you mean?
    Qu'est-ce que cela veut dire? / What does that mean?

- Conditional

    Je voudrais un café crème, s'il vous plaît. / I would like coffee
        with cream, please.

- Imperative

    Veuillez vous asseoir. / Kindly sit down.
    Veuillez accepter mes meilleurs sentiments. / Please accept my
        best regards.

SAVOIR / TO KNOW (a fact)

- Present

    Je sais la réponse. / I know the answer.
    Je sais lire en français. / I know how to read in French.

- Conditional

  Sauriez-vous où est le docteur? / Would you know where the
  doctor is?
  Je ne saurais penser à tout! / I can't think of everything!

- Imperative

  Sachons-le bien! / Let's be well aware of it!
  Sachez que votre père vient de mourir. / Be informed that your
  father has just died.

SAVOIR AND CONNAÎTRE
The main difference between the meaning of these two
verbs in the sense of "to know" is that *connaître* means
merely to be acquainted with; for example, to be acquainted
with a person, a city, a neighborhood, a country, the title of
a book, the works of an author.

  Savez-vous la réponse? / Do you know the answer?
  Savez-vous quelle heure il est? / Do you know what time it is?
  Connaissez-vous cette dame? / Do you know this lady?
  Connaissez-vous Paris? / Do you know Paris?
  Connaissez-vous ce livre? / Do you know this book?

ENTENDRE AND COMPRENDRE
The main difference between the meaning of these two
verbs is that *entendre* means "to hear" and *comprendre*
"to understand." Sometimes *entendre* can mean "to
understand" or "to mean."

  Entendez-vous la musique? / Do you hear the music?
  Comprenez-vous la leçon? / Do you understand the lesson?
  "M'entends-tu?!" dit la mère à l'enfant. "Ne fais pas cela!" /
  "Do you understand me?!" says the mother to the child.
  "Don't do that!"
  *Je ne comprends pas le docteur Fu Manchu parce qu'il ne parle
  que chinois.* / I do not understand Dr. Fu Manchu because he
  speaks only Chinese.
  Qu'entendez-vous par là? / What do you mean by that? What
  are you insinuating by that remark?
  *Je vous entends, mais je ne vous comprends pas; expliquez-
  vous, s'il vous plaît.* / I hear you, but I don't understand you;
  explain yourself, please.

QUITTER, PARTIR, SORTIR, AND LAISSER

These four verbs all mean "to leave," but note the differences in their uses:

- Use *quitter* when you state a direct object noun or pronoun that could be a person or a place.

    J'ai quitté mes amis devant le théâtre. / I left my friends in front of the theater.
    J'ai quitté la maison à six heures du matin. / I left the house at six in the morning.

- Use *partir* when there is no direct object noun or pronoun.

    Elle est partie tout de suite. / She left immediately.

    However, if you use the preposition *de* after *partir,* you may add a direct object, but it would be object of the preposition *de,* not of the verb *partir.*

    Elle est partie de la maison à six heures du matin. / She left (from) the house at six in the morning.

- Use *sortir,* in the sense of "to go out." With no direct object:

    Elle est sortie il y a une heure. / She went out an hour ago.

    However, if you use the preposition *de* after *sortir,* you may add a direct object, but it would be object of the preposition *de,* not of the verb *sortir.*

    Elle est sortie de la maison il y a une heure. / She left (went out of) the house an hour ago.

    Note that *sortir* can also be conjugated with *avoir* to form a compound tense, but then the meaning changes because it can take a direct object.

    Elle a sorti son mouchoir pour se moucher. / She took out her handkerchief to wipe her nose.
    Elle a sorti son mouchoir pour moucher son enfant. / She took out her handkerchief to wipe her child's nose.

- Use *laisser* when you leave behind something that is not stationary; in other words, something movable, for example, books and articles of clothing.

    J'ai laissé mes livres sur la table dans la cuisine. / I left my books on the table in the kitchen.
    J'ai laissé mon imperméable à la maison. / I left my raincoat at home.

Note that *laisser* also has the meaning "to let, allow a person to do something":

J'ai laissé mon ami partir. / I let (allowed) my friend to leave.

| Mnemonic tip | *Partir* / to leave, go away contains an *a* and so does "away." *Sortir* / to go out contains an *o* and so does "out." |

FALLOIR

• Falloir is an impersonal verb, which means that it is used only in the third person singular (*il* form) in all the tenses; its primary meaning is "to be necessary."

Il faut étudier pour avoir de bonnes notes. / It is necessary to study in order to have good grades.
Faut-il le faire tout de suite? / Is it necessary to do it at once?
Oui, il le faut. / Yes, it is (understood: necessary to do it).

The use of the neuter direct object *le* is needed to show emphasis and to complete the thought.

Il faut être honnête. / It is necessary to be honest.

In the negative:

Il ne faut pas être malhonnête. / One must not be dishonest.

Note that *il faut* in the negative means "one must not."

Il ne faut pas fumer à l'école. / One must not smoke in school.

§7.12 OTHER VERBS WITH SPECIAL MEANINGS

arriver / to happen   *Qu'est-ce qui est arrivé?* / What happened?
avoir / to have something the matter   *Qu'est-ce que vous avez?* / What's the matter with you?
entendre dire que / to hear it said that, hear that   *J'entends dire que Robert s'est marié.* / I hear that Robert got married.
entendre parler de / to hear of, about   *J'ai entendu parler d'un grand changement dans l'administration.* / I've heard about a big change in the administration.
envoyer chercher / to send for   *Je vais envoyer chercher le médecin.* / I'm going to send for the doctor.

être à quelqu'un / to belong to someone   *Ce livre est à moi.* / This book belongs to me.

faillir + infinitive   to almost do something   *Le bébé a failli tomber.* / The baby almost fell.

mettre / to put on   *Gisèle a mis sa plus jolie robe.* / Gisèle put on her prettiest dress.

mettre la table / to set the table

profiter de / to take advantage of

rendre visite à / to pay a visit to

venir à / to happen to   *Si nous venons à nous rencontrer, nous pourrons prendre une tasse de café.* / If we happen to meet each other, we can have a cup of coffee.

venir de + infinitive / to have just done something   *Joseph vient de partir.* / Joseph has just left; *Barbara venait de partir quand Françoise est arrivée.* / Barbara had just left when Françoise arrived.

§7.13 INFINITIVES

- In English, an *infinitive* contains the preposition "to" in front of it: "to give," "to finish," "to sell." In French an infinitive has a certain ending. There are three major types of infinitives in French: those that end in *-er (donner);* those that end in *-ir (finir);* and those that end in *-re (vendre).*

- Make an infinitive negative in French by placing *ne pas* in front of it.

  Je vous dis de ne pas sortir. / I am telling you not to go out.

- The infinitive is often used after a verb of perception to express an action that is in progress.

  J'entends quelqu'un chanter. / I hear somebody singing.
  Je vois venir les enfants. / I see the children coming.

  Some common verbs of perception are: *apercevoir* / to perceive, *écouter* / to listen to, *entendre* / to hear, *regarder* / to look at, *sentir* / to feel, *voir* / to see.

- There are certain French verbs that take either the preposition *à* or *de* + infinitive.

  Il commence à pleuvoir. / It is beginning to rain.
  Il a cessé de pleuvoir. / It has stopped raining.

- *Avant de* and *sans* + infinitive

  Sylvie a mangé avant de sortir. / Sylvia ate before going out.
  André est parti sans dire un mot. / Andrew left without saying a word.

- Use of infinitive instead of a verb form

  Generally speaking, an infinitive is used instead of a verb form if the subject in a sentence is the same for the actions expressed.

  Je veux faire le travail. / I want to do the work.

  BUT if there are two different subjects, you must use a new clause and a new verb form.

  Je veux que vous fassiez le travail. / I want you to do the work.
  Je préfère me coucher tôt. / I prefer to go to bed early.

  BUT

  Je préfère que vous vous couchiez tôt. / I prefer that you go to bed early.

- Past infinitive

  In French the past infinitive is expressed by using the infinitive form of *avoir* or *être* + the past participle of the main verb being used.

  Après avoir quitté la maison, Monsieur et Madame Dubé sont allés au cinéma. / After leaving the house, Mr. and Mrs. Dubé went to the movies.
  Après être arrivée, Jeanne a téléphoné à sa mère. / After arriving, Jeanne telephoned her mother.

§7.14 CAUSATIVE (CAUSAL) FAIRE

The construction *faire* + infinitive means to have something done by someone. The causative *faire* can be in any tense, but it must be followed by an infinitive.

Examples with nouns and pronouns as direct and indirect objects:

Madame Smith fait travailler ses élèves dans la classe de français. / Mrs. Smith makes her students work in French class.

In this example, the direct object is the noun *élèves* and it is placed right after the infinitive.

Madame Smith les fait travailler dans la classe de français. /
Mrs. Smith makes them work (has them work) in French class.

In this example, the direct object is the pronoun *les*, referring to *les élèves*. It is placed in front of the verb form of *faire*, where it logically belongs.

Madame Smith fait lire la phrase. / Mrs.Smith is having the sentence read. OR Mrs. Smith has the sentence read.

In this example, the direct object is the noun *phrase* and it is placed right after the infinitive, as in the first example.

Madame Smith la fait lire. / Mrs. Smith is having it read.

In this example, the direct object is the pronoun *la*, referring to *la phrase*. It is placed in front of the verb form of *faire*, where it logically belongs. This is like the second example, but here the direct object is a thing. In the other two examples, the direct object is a person.

§7.15 SUBJUNCTIVE

The subjunctive is not a tense, but a *mood,* or mode. Usually when we speak in French or English, we use the indicative mood but the subjunctive mood in French must be used in specific cases. They are:

After Certain Conjunctions

When the following conjunctions introduce a new clause, the verb in that new clause is usually in the subjunctive mood.

à condition que / on condition that
à moins que / unless
afin que / in order that, so that
attendre que / to wait until
au cas que; en cas que / in case
bien que / although
de crainte que / for fear that
de peur que / for fear that
de sorte que / so that
en attendant que / until
jusqu'à ce que / until
malgré que / although
pour que / in order that
pourvu que / provided that
quoique / although

Je vous explique pour que vous compreniez. / I am explaining to you so that you will understand.

Attendez que je finisse mon dîner / Wait until I finish my dinner.

Au cas que nous soyons d'accord . . . / In case we are in agreement . . .

En cas qu'il vienne, soyez prêts. / In case he comes, be ready.

After Indefinite Expressions

> *où que* / wherever
> *quel que* / whatever
> *qui que* / whoever
> *quoi que* / whatever, no matter what

After an Indefinite Antecedent

The subjunctive is needed after an indefinite antecedent because the person or thing desired may possibly not exist; or, if it does exist, you may never find it.

Je cherche une personne qui soit honnête. / I am looking for a person who is honest.

Je cherche un appartement qui ne soit pas trop cher. / I am looking for an apartment that is not too expensive.

Connaissez-vous quelqu'un qui puisse réparer mon téléviseur une fois pour toutes? / Do you know someone who can repair my TV set once and for all?

Y a-t-il un élève qui comprenne le subjonctif? / Is there a student who understands the subjunctive?

After a Superlative Expressing an Opinion

> The most common superlatives expressing an opinion are: *le seul (la seule)* / the only, *le premier (la première)* / the first, *le dernier (la dernière)* / the last, *le plus petit (la plus petite)* / the smallest, *le plus grand (la plus grande)* / the biggest

A mon avis, Marie est la seule étudiante qui comprenne le subjonctif. / In my opinion, Mary is the only student who understands the subjunctive.

Selon mon opinion, Henriette est l'élève la plus jolie que j'aie jamais vue. / According to my opinion, Henrietta is the prettiest pupil I have ever seen.

After *que,* Meaning "Let" or "May"

The subjunctive is required after *que* to express a wish, an order, or a command in the third person singular or plural.

Qu'il parte! / Let him leave!
Que Dieu nous pardonne! / May God forgive us!
Qu'ils s'en aillent! / Let them go away!

After Certain Impersonal Expressions

c'est dommage que / it's a pity that
il est bizarre que / it is odd that
il est bon que / it is good that
il est douteux que / it is doubtful that
il est essentiel que / it is essential that
il est étonnant que / it is astonishing that
il est étrange que / it is strange that
il est heureux que / it is fortunate that
il est honteux que / it is a shame that
il est important que / it is important that
il est impossible que / it is impossible that
il est nécessaire que / it is necessary that
il est possible que / it is possible that
il est regrettable que / it is regrettable that
il est temps que / it is time that
il est urgent que / it is urgent that
il faut que / it is necessary that
il se peut que / it may be that
il semble que / it seems that
il vaut mieux que / it is better that

After Certain Verbs Expressing Doubt, Emotion, or Wishing

aimer que / to like that
aimer mieux que / to prefer that
s'attendre à ce que / to expect that
avoir peur que / to be afraid that
craindre que / to fear that
défendre que / to forbid that

désirer que / to desire that
douter que / to doubt that
empêcher que / to prevent that
s'étonner que / to be astonished that
être bien aise que / to be pleased that
être content que / to be glad that
être désolé que / to be distressed that
être étonné que / to be astonished that
être heureux que / to be happy that
être joyeux que / to be joyful that
être ravi que / to be delighted that
être triste que / to be sad that
exiger que / to demand that
se fâcher que / to be angry that
insister que / to insist that
ordonner que / to order that
préférer que / to prefer that
regretter que / to regret that
souhaiter que / to wish that
tenir à ce que / to insist upon
vouloir que / to want

EXAMPLES

J'aimerais que vous restiez ici. / I would like you to stay here.
J'aime mieux que vous restiez ici. / I prefer that you stay here.
Nous nous attendons à ce qu'elle vienne immédiatement. / We
  expect her to come immediately.
Ta mère est contente que tu sois heureux. / Your mother is glad
  that you are happy.

After Verbs of Believing and Thinking

Such verbs are *croire, penser, trouver* (meaning "to think,
to have an impression"), and *espérer* when used in the
negative or interrogative.

Je ne pense pas qu'il soit coupable. / I don't think that he is guilty.
Croyez-vous qu'il dise la vérité? / Do you believe he is telling
  the truth?
*Trouvez-vous qu'il y ait beaucoup de crimes dans la société
d'aujourd'hui?* / Do you find (think) that there are many crimes
  in today's society?

§7.16 SUMMARY OF TENSES AND MOODS

The 7 simple tenses	The 7 compound tenses
Present indicative	Past indefinite *(passé composé)*
Imperfect indicative	Pluperfect indicative
Past definite	Past anterior
Future	Future perfect
Conditional present	Conditional perfect
Present subjunctive	Past subjunctive
Imperfect subjunctive	Pluperfect subjunctive
	Imperative or Command

§7.17 SPELLING IRREGULARITIES OF SOME COMMON VERBS

The verbs conjugated here all undergo certain spelling changes in the tenses indicated.*

The subject pronouns have been omitted in order to eliminate repetition and to emphasize the verb forms. They are:

	Singular	Plural
1st	*je (j')*	*nous*
2d	*tu*	*vous*
3d	*il, elle, on*	*ils, elles*

PRESENT INDICATIVE

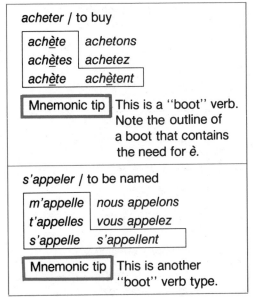

acheter / to buy

achète	*achetons*
achètes	*achetez*
achète	*achètent*

| Mnemonic tip | This is a "boot" verb. Note the outline of a boot that contains the need for è. |

s'appeler / to be named

m'appelle	*nous appelons*
t'appelles	*vous appelez*
s'appelle	*s'appellent*

| Mnemonic tip | This is another "boot" verb type. |

For additional verb conjugations, see *501 French Verbs* by Christopher Kendris, ©1982 by Barron's Educational Series, Inc.

apprendre / to learn

apprends	apprenons
apprends	apprenez
apprend	apprennent

boire / to drink

bois	buvons
bois	buvez
boit	boivent

Mnemonic tip	This too is a "boot" verb. Note the "*s, s, t*" pattern in the singular.

commencer / to begin, start

commence	commençons
commences	commencez
commence	commencent

comprendre / to understand (like *prendre;* add *com* at the beginning of *prendre*)

conduire / to drive; to lead

conduis	conduisons
conduis	conduisez
conduit	conduisent

connaître / to know, to be acquainted with

connais	connaissons
connais	connaissez
connaît	connaissent

courir / to run

cours	courons
cours	courez
court	courent

croire / to believe

crois	croyons
crois	croyez
croit	croient

devenir / to become

deviens	devenons
deviens	devenez
devient	deviennent

devoir / to owe; to have to

dois	devons
dois	devez
doit	doivent

dire / to say; to tell

dis	disons
dis	dites
dit	disent

dormir / to sleep

dors	dormons
dors	dormez
dort	dorment

écrire / to write

écris	écrivons
écris	écrivez
écrit	écrivent

envoyer / to send

envoie	envoyons
envoies	envoyez
envoie	envoient

espérer / to hope

espère	espérons
espères	espérez
espère	espèrent

falloir / to be necessary

il faut

se lever / to get up

me lève	nous levons
te lèves	vous levez
se lève	se lèvent

lire / to read

lis	lisons
lis	lisez
lit	lisent

manger / to eat

mange	mang<u>e</u>ons
manges	mangez
mange	mangent

mettre / to place, put; to put on

mets	mettons
mets	mettez
met	mettent

mourir / to die

meur<u>s</u>	mourons
meur<u>s</u>	mourez
meur<u>t</u>	meuren<u>t</u>

nager / to swim

nage	nag<u>e</u>ons
nages	nagez
nage	nagent

naître / to be born

nais	naissons
nais	naissez
naît	naissent

offrir / to offer

offre	offrons
offres	offrez
offre	offrent

ouvrir / to open

ouvre	ouvrons
ouvres	ouvrez
ouvre	ouvrent

partir / to leave

pars	partons
pars	partez
part	partent

pleuvoir / to rain

il pleut

pouvoir / to be able, can

peu<u>x</u> OR pui<u>s</u>	pouvons
peu<u>x</u>	pouvez
peu<u>t</u>	peuven<u>t</u>

préférer / to prefer

préf<u>è</u>re	préférons
préf<u>è</u>res	préférez
préf<u>è</u>re	préf<u>è</u>rent

prendre / to take

prends	prenons
prends	prenez
prend	prennent

protéger / to protect

prot<u>è</u>ge	protégeons
prot<u>è</u>ges	protégez
prot<u>è</u>ge	prot<u>è</u>gent

recevoir / to receive

reçoi<u>s</u>	recevons
reçoi<u>s</u>	recevez
reçoi<u>t</u>	reçoiven<u>t</u>

revenir / to return, come back (like *venir;* add *re-* at the beginning of *venir*)

rire / to laugh

ris	rions
ris	riez
rit	rient

savoir / to know (a fact)

sais	savons
sais	savez
sait	savent

servir / to serve

sers	*servons*
sers	*servez*
sert	*servent*

sortir / to go out; to leave

sors	*sortons*
sors	*sortez*
sort	*sortent*

tenir / to hold

tiens	*tenons*
tiens	*tenez*
tient	*tiennent*

venir / to come

viens	*venons*
viens	*venez*
vient	*viennent*

vivre / to live

vis	*vivons*
vis	*vivez*
vit	*vivent*

voir / to see

vois	*voyons*
vois	*voyez*
voit	*voient*

vouloir / to want

veux	*voulons*
veux	*voulez*
veut	*veulent*

voyager / to travel

voyage	*voyageons*
voyages	*voyagez*
voyage	*voyagent*

IMPERFECT INDICATIVE

---

apprendre / to learn

apprenais	apprenions
apprenais	appreniez
apprenait	apprenaient

---

boire / to drink

buvais	buvions
buvais	buviez
buvait	buvaient

---

commencer / to begin, to start

commençais	commencions
commençais	commenciez
commençait	commençaient

---

comprendre / to understand (like *prendre;* add *com* at the beginning of *prendre*)

---

conduire / to drive; to lead

conduisais	conduisions
conduisais	conduisiez
conduisait	conduisaient

---

connaître / to know, be acquainted with

connaissais	connaissions
connaissais	connaissiez
connaissait	connaissaient

---

courir / to run

courais	courions
courais	couriez
courait	couraient

---

croire / to believe

croyais	croyions
croyais	croyiez
croyait	croyaient

---

devenir / to become

devenais	devenions
devenais	deveniez
devenait	devenaient

devoir / to owe; to have to

devais	*devions*
devais	*deviez*
devait	*devaient*

dire / to say; to tell

disais	*disions*
disais	*disiez*
disait	*disaient*

dormir / to sleep

dormais	*dormions*
dormais	*dormiez*
dormais	*dormaient*

écrire / to write

écrivais	*écrivions*
écrivais	*écriviez*
écrivait	*écrivaient*

falloir / to be necessary

il fallait

lire / to read

lisais	*lisions*
lisais	*lisiez*
lisait	*lisaient*

manger / to eat

mangeais	*mangions*
mangeais	*mangiez*
mangeait	*mangeaient*

mourir / to die

mourais	*mourions*
mourais	*mouriez*
mourait	*mouraient*

nager / to swim

nageais	*nagions*
nageais	*nagiez*
nageait	*nageaient*

naître / to be born

naissais	*naissions*
naissais	*naissiez*
naissait	*naissaient*

offrir / to offer

offrais	*offrions*
offrais	*offriez*
offrait	*offraient*

ouvrir / to open

ouvrais	*ouvrions*
ouvrais	*ouvriez*
ouvrait	*ouvraient*

partir / to leave

partais	*partions*
partais	*partiez*
partait	*partaient*

pleuvoir / to rain

il pleuvait

prendre / to take

prenais	*prenions*
prenais	*preniez*
prenait	*prenaient*

protéger / to protect

protégeais	*protégions*
protégeais	*protégiez*
protégeait	*protégeaient*

revenir / to return, to come back
(like *venir;* add *re* at the beginning of *venir*)

rire / to laugh

riais	*riions*
riais	*riiez*
riait	*riaient*

savoir / to know (a fact)

savais	savions
savais	saviez
savait	savaient

servir / to serve

servais	servions
servais	serviez
servait	servaient

sortir / to go out; to leave

sortais	sortions
sortais	sortiez
sortait	sortaient

tenir / to hold

tenais	tenions
tenais	teniez
tenait	tenaient

venir / to come

venais	venions
venais	veniez
venait	venaient

vivre / to live

vivais	vivions
vivais	viviez
vivait	vivaient

voir / to see

voyais	voyions
voyais	voyiez
voyait	voyaient

vouloir / to want

voulais	voulions
voulais	vouliez
voulait	voulaient

voyager / to travel

voyageais	voyagions
voyageais	voyagiez
voyageait	voyageaient

§7.18 BASIC NEGATIONS OF VERBS

The common negations of verbs are *ne* + verb + any of the following:

aucun, aucune / no, not one, not any

> *Je n'ai aucun livre.* / I have no book.
> *Robert n'a aucune amie.* / Robert has no girlfriend.

guère / hardly, scarcely

> *Paul ne parle guère.* / Paul hardly (scarcely) talks.

jamais / never

> *Jean n'étudie jamais.* / John never studies.

ni . . . ni / neither . . . nor

> *Je n'ai ni argent ni billet.* / I have neither money nor tickets.

nul, nulle / no, not any

> *Je n'en ai nul besoin.* / I have no need of it.
> *Je ne vais nulle part.* / I'm not going anywhere.

pas / not

> *Je n'ai pas de papier.* / I haven't any paper.

pas du tout / not at all

> *Je ne comprends pas du tout.* / I do not understand at all.

personne / nobody, no one, not anybody

> *Je ne vois personne.* / I don't see anybody. I see no one.

plus / any longer, no more, not any more

> *Mon père ne travaille plus.* / My father doesn't work any more.

point / not at all

Cet enfant n'a point d'argent. / This child has no money at all.

que / only, but only

Je n'ai que deux francs. / I have (but) only two francs.

rien / nothing

Je n'ai rien sur moi. / I have nothing on me.

Note that all these negations require *ne* in front of the main verb. Also note that *aucun, aucune, nul, nulle, personne, rien* can be used as subjects and you still need to use *ne* in front of the verb.

Personne n'entend le bruit. / Nobody hears the noise.
Rien n'est jamais parfait. / Nothing is ever perfect.

Une devinette / a riddle

J'ai des yeux mais je n'ai pas de paupières et je vis dans l'eau. Qui suis-je? / I have eyes but I don't have eyelids and I live in the water. Who am I?

un poisson

---

§7.19 FOUR CONJUGATED VERBS

The following verbs—*aller, avoir, être,* and *faire*—have been fully conjugated in all their tenses because they are so frequently used.

aller / to go
Present participle: *allant*   Past participle: *allé(e)(s)*

THE SEVEN SIMPLE TENSES		THE SEVEN COMPOUND TENSES	
Singular	**Plural**	**Singular**	**Plural**
Present indicative		Past indefinite	
vais	allons	suis allé(e)	sommes allé(e)s
vas	allez	es allé(e)	êtes allé(e)(s)
va	vont	est allé(e)	sont allé(e)s
Imperfect indicative		Pluperfect OR Past perfect indicative	
allais	allions	étais allé(e)	étions allé(e)s
allais	alliez	étais allé(e)	étiez allé(e)(s)
allait	allaient	était allé(e)	étaient allé(e)s
Past definite		Past anterior	
allai	allâmes	fus allé(e)	fûmes allé(e)s
allas	allâtes	fus allé(e)	fûtes allé(e)(s)
alla	allèrent	fut allé(e)	furent allé(e)s
Future		Future perfect OR Future anterior	
irai	irons	serai allé(e)	serons allé(e)s
iras	irez	seras allé(e)	serez allé(e)(s)
ira	iront	sera allé(e)	seront allé(e)s
Conditional		Conditional perfect	
irais	irions	serais allé(e)	serions allé(e)s
irais	iriez	serais allé(e)	seriez allé(e)(s)
irait	iraient	serait allé(e)	seraient allé(e)s
Present subjunctive		Past subjunctive	
aille	allions	sois allé(e)	soyons allé(e)s
ailles	alliez	sois allé(e)	soyez allé(e)(s)
aille	aillent	soit allé(e)	soient allé(e)s
Imperfect subjunctive		Pluperfect OR Past perfect subjunctive	
allasse	allassions	fusse allé(e)	fussions allé(e)s
allasses	allassiez	fusses allé(e)	fussiez allé(e)(s)
allât	allassent	fût allé(e)	fussent allé(e)s

Imperative OR Command
va
allons
allez

Common idiomatic expressions using this verb:

Comment allez-vous? / Je vais bien (mal) (mieux).

aller à la pêche / to go fishing
aller à la rencontre de quelqu'un / to go to meet someone
aller à pied / to walk, to go on foot
aller au fond des choses / to get to the bottom of things
Ça va? / Is everything OK? *Oui, ça va!* / Yes, everything's OK.

For more idioms using *aller*, see §12.2.

| Mnemonic tip | *Un ver vert va vers un verre vert.* |

A green worm is going toward a green glass.

The words *ver, vers, vert, verre* are all pronounced the same as *ver* in the English word "very."

avoir / to have
Present participle: *ayant*   Past participle: *eu*

THE SEVEN SIMPLE TENSES		THE SEVEN COMPOUND TENSES	
Singular	**Plural**	**Singular**	**Plural**
Present indicative		Past indefinite	
ai	*avons*	*ai eu*	*avons eu*
as	*avez*	*as eu*	*avez eu*
a	*ont*	*a eu*	*ont eu*
Imperfect indicative		Pluperfect OR Past perfect indicative	
avais	*avions*	*avais eu*	*avions eu*
avais	*aviez*	*avais eu*	*aviez eu*
avait	*avaient*	*avait eu*	*avaient eu*
Past definite		Past anterior	
eus	*eûmes*	*eus eu*	*eûmes eu*
eus	*eûtes*	*eus eu*	*eûtes eu*
eut	*eurent*	*eut eu*	*eurent eu*
Future		Future perfect OR Future anterior	
aurai	*aurons*	*aurai eu*	*aurons eu*
auras	*aurez*	*auras eu*	*aurez eu*
aura	*auront*	*aura eu*	*auront eu*
Conditional		Conditional perfect	
aurais	*aurions*	*aurais eu*	*aurions eu*
aurais	*auriez*	*aurais eu*	*auriez eu*
aurait	*auraient*	*aurait eu*	*auraient eu*
Present subjunctive		Past subjunctive	
aie	*ayons*	*aie eu*	*ayons eu*
aies	*ayez*	*aies eu*	*ayez eu*
ait	*aient*	*ait eu*	*aient eu*
Imperfect subjunctive		Pluperfect OR Past perfect subjunctive	
eusse	*eussions*	*eusse eu*	*eussions eu*
eusses	*eussiez*	*eusses eu*	*eussiez eu*
eût	*eussent*	*eût eu*	*eussent eu*

Imperative OR Command
aie
ayons
ayez

Common idiomatic expressions using this verb:

avoir . . . ans / to be . . . years old
avoir à + infinitive / to have to, to be obliged to + inf.
avoir besoin de / to need, to have need of
avoir chaud / to be (feel) warm (persons)
avoir froid / to be (feel) cold (persons)
avoir sommeil / to be (feel) sleepy

avoir quelque chose à faire / to have something to do
avoir de la chance / to be lucky
avoir faim / to be hungry
avoir soif / to be thirsty
avoir honte / to be (feel) ashamed

For more idioms using *avoir*, see §12.2.

être / to be
Present participle: *étant*   Past participle: *été*

THE SEVEN SIMPLE TENSES		THE SEVEN COMPOUND TENSES	
Singular	**Plural**	**Singular**	**Plural**
Present indicative		Past indefinite	
suis	sommes	ai été	avons été
es	êtes	as été	avez été
est	sont	a été	ont été
Imperfect indicative		Pluperfect OR Past perfect indicative	
étais	étions	avais été	avions été
étais	étiez	avais été	aviez été
était	étaient	avait été	avaient été
Past definite		Past anterior	
fus	fûmes	eus été	eûmes été
fus	fûtes	eus été	eûtes été
fut	furent	eut été	eurent été
Future		Future perfect OR Future anterior	
serai	serons	aurai été	aurons été
seras	serez	auras été	aurez été
sera	seront	aura été	auront été
Conditional		Conditional perfect	
serais	serions	aurais été	aurions été
serais	seriez	aurais été	auriez été
serait	seraient	aurait été	auraient été
Present subjunctive		Past subjunctive	
sois	soyons	aie été	ayons été
sois	soyez	aies été	ayez été
soit	soient	ait été	aient été
Imperfect subjunctive		Pluperfect OR Past perfect subjunctive	
fusse	fussions	eusse été	eussions été
fusses	fussiez	eusses été	eussiez été
fût	fussent	eût été	eussent été

Imperative OR Command
sois
soyons
soyez

Common idiomatic expressions using this verb:

être en train de + infinitive / to be in the act of + present participle, to be in the process of, to be busy + present participle: *Mon père est en train d'écrire une lettre à mes grands-parents.* / My father is writing a letter to my grandparents.

être à l'heure / to be on time	*Je suis à vous.* / I am at your service.
être à temps / to be in time	*Je suis d'avis que . . .* / I am of the opinion that . . .
être pressé(e) / to be in a hurry	*être au courant de* / to be informed about

For more idioms using *être*, see §12.2.

faire / to do, to make
Present participle: *faisant*   Past participle: *fait*

THE SEVEN SIMPLE TENSES		THE SEVEN COMPOUND TENSES	
Singular	**Plural**	**Singular**	**Plural**
Present indicative		Past indefinite	
fais	faisons	ai fait	avons fait
fais	faites	as fait	avez fait
fait	font	a fait	ont fait
Imperfect indicative		Pluperfect OR Past perfect indicative	
faisais	faisions	avais fait	avions fait
faisais	faisiez	avais fait	aviez fait
faisait	faisaient	avait fait	avaient fait
Past definite		Past anterior	
fis	fîmes	eus fait	eûmes fait
fis	fîtes	eus fait	eûtes fait
fit	firent	eut fait	eurent fait
Future		Future perfect OR Future anterior	
ferai	ferons	aurai fait	aurons fait
feras	ferez	auras fait	aurez fait
fera	feront	aura fait	auront fait
Conditional		Conditional perfect	
ferais	ferions	aurais fait	aurions fait
ferais	feriez	aurais fait	auriez fait
ferait	feraient	aurait fait	auraient fait
Present subjunctive		Past subjunctive	
fasse	fassions	aie fait	ayons fait
fasses	fassiez	aies fait	ayez fait
fasse	fassent	ait fait	aient fait
Imperfect subjunctive		Pluperfect OR Past perfect subjunctive	
fisse	fissions	eusse fait	eussions fait
fisses	fissiez	eusses fait	eussiez fait
fît	fissent	eût fait	eussent fait

Imperative OR Command
fais
faisons
faites

Common idiomatic expressions using this verb:

faire beau / to be beautiful weather
faire chaud / to be warm weather
faire froid / to be cold weather
faire de l'autostop / to hitchhike
faire attention à quelqu'un ou à quelque chose / to pay attention to someone or something

For more idioms using *faire*, see §12.2.

§8.

Adverbs

DEFINITION

An *adverb* is a word that modifies a verb, an adjective, or another adverb.

§8.1
FORMATION

Many French adverbs are not formed from another word, for example: *bien, mal, vite, combien, comment, pourquoi, où.*

There are many other adverbs that are formed from another word. The usual way is to add the suffix *-ment* to the masculine singular form of an adjective whose last letter is a vowel; for example: *probable, probablement; poli, poliment; vrai, vraiment.*

The suffix *-ment* is added to the feminine singular form if the masculine singular ends in a consonant; for example: *affreux, affreuse, affreusement; seul, seule, seulement; amer, amère, amèrement; franc, franche, franchement.*

The ending *-ment* is equivalent to the English ending "-ly": *lent, lente, lentement* / slow, slowly.

Some adjectives that end in *-ant* or *-ent* become adverbs by changing *-ant* to *-amment* and *-ent* to *-emment: innocent, innocemment; constant, constamment; récent, récemment.*

Some adverbs take *é* instead of *e* before adding *-ment: profond, profondément; confus, confusément; précis, précisément.*

The adjective *gentil* becomes *gentiment* as an adverb and *bref* becomes *brièvement.*

§8.2
POSITION

1. *David aime beaucoup les chocolats.*
2. *Paulette a parlé distinctement.*
3. *Julie a bien parlé.*

- In French, an adverb ordinarily follows the simple verb it modifies, as in the first model sentence above.
- If a verb is compound, as in the *past indefinite* (sentence 2), the adverb generally follows the past participle if it is a long adverb. The adverb *distinctement* is long. Some exceptions: *certainement, complètement,* and *probablement* are usually placed between the helping verb and the past participle: *Elle est probablement partie. Il a complètement fini le travail.*

111

- If a verb is compound, as in the *past indefinite* (sentence 3), short common adverbs (like *beaucoup, bien, déjà, encore, mal, mieux, souvent, toujours*) ordinarily precede the past participle; in other words, they may be placed between the helping verb and the past participle.
- For emphasis, an adverb may be placed at the beginning of a sentence: *Malheureusement, Suzanne est déjà partie.*

§8.3
TYPES
§8.3–1
Interrogative Adverbs

Some common interrogative adverbs are *comment, combien, pourquoi, quand, où.*

EXAMPLES
Comment allez-vous? Combien coûte ce livre? Pourquoi partez-vous? Quand arriverez-vous? Où allez-vous?

§8.3–2
Adverbs of Quantity

Some adverbial expressions of quantity are *beaucoup de, assez de, peu de, trop de, plus de.* With these, no article is used: *peu de sucre, beaucoup de travail, assez de temps, trop de lait, combien d'argent.*

§8.3–3
Comparative and Superlative Adverbs

Adverb	Comparative	Superlative
vite / quickly	*plus vite (que) /* more quickly (than) faster (than)	*le plus vite /* (the) most quickly, (the) fastest
	moins vite (que) / less quickly (than)	*le moins vite /* (the) least quickly
	aussi vite (que) / as quickly (as), as fast (as)	

EXAMPLES
Arlette parle plus vite que Marie-France. **/ Arlette speaks faster than Marie-France.**
Madame Legrange parle moins vite que Madame Duval. **/ Madame Legrange speaks less quickly than Madame Duval.**
Monsieur Bernard parle aussi vite que Monsieur Claude. **/ Monsieur Bernard speaks as fast as Monsieur Claude.**

Madame Durocher parle le plus vite tandis que Madame Milot parle le moins vite. / Madame Durocher speaks the fastest whereas Madame Milot speaks the least fast (the slowest).
Aussi . . . que becomes *si . . . que* in a negative sentence.

EXAMPLE

Justin ne parle pas si vite que Justine. / Justin does not talk as fast as Justine.

Irregular Comparative and Superlative Adverbs

Adverb	Comparative	Superlative
bien / well	*mieux* / better	*le mieux* / best, the best
beaucoup / much	*plus* / more	*le plus* / most, the most
mal / badly	{ *plus mal* / worse { *pis* / worse	{ *le plus mal* / worst, the worst { *le moins bien* / the worst { *le pis* / worst, the worst
peu / little	*moins* / less	*le moins* / least, the least

EXAMPLES

Pierre travaille bien, Henri travaille mieux que Robert et Georges travaille le mieux.
Marie étudie beaucoup, Paulette étudie plus que Marie, et Henriette étudie le plus.

§8.4
OUI AND *SI*

Ordinarily, *oui* is used to mean "yes." However, *si* can also be used to mean "yes" in response to a question in the negative.

EXAMPLES

Aimez-vous le français?—Oui, j'aime le français.
N'aimez-vous pas le français?—Si, j'aime le français.

Mnemonic tip | *Une scie* (pronounced like the English "see") is a carpenter's "saw."

§9.

Prepositions — Special Uses

Dans and *en* + a length of time

These two prepositions mean "in," but each is used in a different sense.

Dans + a length of time indicates that something will happen *at the end* of that length of time.

> *Le docteur va venir dans une demi-heure.* / The doctor will come in a half-hour (i.e., at the end of a half-hour).

Dans and a duration of time can be at the beginning of the sentence or at the end of it and future time is ordinarily implied.

En + a length of time indicates that something happened or will happen at any time *within* that length of time.

EXAMPLES
Robert a fait cela en une heure. / Robert did that in (within) an (one) hour.
Robert fera cela en une heure. / Robert will do that in (within) an (one) hour.

BUT

Robert fera cela dans une heure. / Robert will do that in (at the end of) an (one) hour.

Envers and *vers*

Envers is used in a figurative sense in the meaning of "with regard to" someone, "with respect to" someone, "for" someone, or "for" something.

EXAMPLES
Je montre beaucoup de respect envers les vieilles personnes. / I show a lot of respect toward old persons.
Je ne montre aucun respect envers un criminel. / I show no respect toward a criminal.

Vers also means "toward," but is used in the physical sense (in the direction of) as well as in the figurative sense.

EXAMPLES

Pourquoi allez-vous vers la porte? / Why are you going toward the door?

Je vais partir vers trois heures. / I am going to leave toward (around) three o'clock.

§9.3   *Pendant* and *pour*

IN THE PRESENT TENSE

Combien de temps étudiez-vous chaque soir? / How long do you study every evening?

J'étudie une heure chaque soir. / I study one hour each night. OR *J'étudie pendant une heure chaque soir.* / I study for one hour each night.

IN THE PAST INDEFINITE

Combien de temps êtes-vous resté(e) à Paris? / How long did you stay in Paris?

Je suis resté(e) à Paris deux semaines. / I stayed in Paris two weeks. OR *Je suis resté(e) à Paris pendant deux semaines.* / I stayed in Paris for two weeks.

IN THE FUTURE

Combien de temps resterez-vous à Paris? / How long will you stay in Paris?

J'y resterai pendant deux semaines. / I will stay there for two weeks. OR *J'y resterai deux semaines.* / I will stay there two weeks.

§10.

Conjunctions

DEFINITION

A conjunction is a word that connects words, phrases, clauses, or sentences, such as *et* / and, *mais* / but, *ou* / or, *parce que* / because. The following is a list of the most common conjunctions.

Basic Conjunctions:

à moins que / unless
afin que / in order that, so that
aussitôt que / as soon as
avant que ' before
bien que / although
car / for
comme / as, since
de crainte que / for fear that
de peur que / for fear that
de sorte que / so that, in such a way that
depuis que / since
dès que / as soon as
donc / therefore, consequently
en même temps que at the same time as

et / and
jusqu'à ce que / until
lorsque / when, at the time when
maintenant que / now that
mais / but
ou / or
parce que / because
pendant le temps que / while
pendant que / while
pour que / in order that
pourvu que / provided that
puisque / since
quand / when
que / that
quoi que / whatever, no matter what
quoique / although
si / if
tandis que / while, whereas

| Mnemonic tip | Pronounce the final <u>c</u> in <u>donc</u> as a *k* when it means consequently (therefore).

Je pense; donc, je suis, I think; therefore, I am.

Special Topics

§11.

Order of Elements in French Sentences

Negative Constructions

Some common negative constructions are *ne* + verb + any of the following:

aucun (aucune) / no, not one, not any

> *Je n'ai aucun livre.* / I have no book.
> *Robert n'a aucune amie.* / Robert has no girlfriend.

guère / hardly, scarcely

> *Paul ne parle guère.* / Paul hardly (scarcely) talks.

jamais / never

> *Jean n'étudie jamais.* / John never studies.

ni . . . ni / neither . . . nor

> *Je n'ai ni argent ni billets.* / I have neither money nor tickets.

nul (nulle) / no, not any

> *Je n'en ai nul besoin.* / I have no need of it.
> *Je ne vais nulle part.* / I'm not going anywhere.

pas / not

> *Je n'ai pas de papier.* / I haven't any paper.

pas du tout / not at all

> *Je ne comprends pas du tout.* / I do not understand at all.

personne / nobody, no one, not anybody

> *Je ne vois personne.* / I don't see anybody. I see no one.

plus / any longer, no more, not anymore

> *Mon père ne travaille plus.* / My father doesn't work anymore.

point / not at all

> *Cet enfant n'a point d'argent.* / This child has no money at all.

que / only, but only

> *Je n'ai que deux francs.* / I have (but) only two francs.

rien / nothing

> *Je n'ai rien sur moi.* / I have nothing on me.

Remember that all these negations require *ne* in front of the main verb. Also note that *aucun (aucune), nul (nulle), personne,* and *rien* can be used as subjects, but you still need to use *ne* in front of the verb.

EXAMPLES
Personne n'est ici. / Nobody is here.
Rien n'est dans ce tiroir. / Nothing is in this drawer.

Une devinette
J'ai des yeux mais je n'ai pas de paupières et je vis dans l'eau. Qui suis-je? / I have eyes, but I don't have eyelids and I live in the water. Who am I?

> *un poisson* / a fish

Declarative Sentence with a Verb in a Simple Tense (e.g., present)

SUBJECT → *ne (n')* +
$$\left\{ \begin{array}{l} me\ (m') \\ te\ (t') \\ se\ (s') \\ nous \\ vous \end{array} \right\} \text{OR} \left\{ \begin{array}{l} le \\ la \\ l' \\ les \end{array} \right\} \text{AND/OR} \left\{ \begin{array}{l} lui \\ leur \end{array} \right\}$$

OR *y* + *en* + **VERB** → *pas*

EXAMPLES
Il ne me les donne pas. / He is not giving them to me.
Je ne le leur donne pas. / I am not giving it to them.
Il n'y en a pas. / There aren't any of them.

Declarative Sentence with a Verb in a Compound Tense (e.g., *passé composé*)

SUBJECT → *ne (n')* +
$\begin{Bmatrix} me\ (m') \\ te\ (t') \\ se\ (s') \\ nous \\ vous \end{Bmatrix}$
OR
$\begin{Bmatrix} le \\ la \\ l' \\ les \end{Bmatrix}$
AND/OR
$\begin{Bmatrix} lui \\ leur \end{Bmatrix}$

OR *y* + *en* + **VERB** → *pas* + past participle
(auxiliary verb
avoir or *être* in
a simple tense)

EXAMPLES

Yvonne ne s'est pas lavée. / Yvonne did not wash herself.
Il ne m'en a pas envoyé. / He did not send any of them to me.
Je ne le lui ai pas donné. / I did not give it to him (to her).
Nous ne vous les avons pas données. / We have not given
them to you.
Ils ne s'en sont pas allés. / They did not go away.

Affirmative Imperative Sentence

VERB +
$\begin{Bmatrix} le \\ la \\ l' \\ les \end{Bmatrix}$
OR
$\begin{Bmatrix} moi\ (m') \\ toi\ (t') \\ nous \\ vous \end{Bmatrix}$
AND/OR
$\begin{Bmatrix} lui \\ leur \end{Bmatrix}$
OR *y* + *en*

EXAMPLES

Donnez-les-leur. / Give them to them.
Assieds-toi. / Sit down.
Allez-vous-en! / Go away!
Apportez-le-moi! / Bring it to me!
Donnez-m'en! / Give me some!
Allez-y! / Go to it! Go there!

Negative Imperative Sentence

$$\textbf{Ne (N')} + \begin{Bmatrix} me\ (m') \\ te\ (t') \\ nous \\ vous \end{Bmatrix} \text{OR} \begin{Bmatrix} le \\ la \\ l' \\ les \end{Bmatrix} \text{OR} \begin{Bmatrix} lui \\ leur \end{Bmatrix} \text{OR } y + en + \textbf{VERB} \rightarrow \textbf{\textit{pas}}$$

EXAMPLES

Ne l'y mettez pas. / Do not put it in it. Do not put it there.
Ne les leur donnez pas. / Do not give them to them.
Ne t'assieds pas! / Don't sit down!
Ne vous en allez pas! / Don't go away!

| Mnemonic tip | Object pronouns fall in the right order if you alphabetize them!

$$\left. \begin{matrix} la \\ le \\ les \end{matrix} \right\} \begin{matrix} + \\ + \end{matrix} \begin{matrix} leur \\ lui \end{matrix}$$

The order is always the same, whether before or after a verb or before an infinitive.

§12.

Idioms

Depuis

- With the present indicative tense
  When an action of some sort began in the past and is still going on in the present, use the present tense with *depuis* + the length of time.

  Je travaille dans ce bureau depuis trois ans. / I have been working in this office for three years.

  > Use *depuis combien de temps* + the present indicative of the verb to ask how long one has been + verb: *Depuis combien de temps travaillez-vous dans ce bureau?* / How long have you been working in this office? *Je travaille dans ce bureau depuis un an.* / I have been working in this office for one year.

- With the imperfect indicative tense
  When an action of some sort began in the past and continued up to another point in the past that you are telling about, use the imperfect indicative tense with depuis + the length of time:

  J'attendais l'autobus depuis vingt minutes quand il est arrivé. / I had been waiting for the bus for twenty minutes when it arrived.

- In a question
  Depuis combien de temps

  Depuis combien de temps attendez-vous l'autobus? / How long have you been waiting for the bus?
  J'attends l'autobus depuis vingt minutes. / I have been waiting for the bus for twenty minutes.

  Note: When you use *depuis combien de temps* in a question, you expect the other person to tell you how long, how much time — how many minutes, how many hours, how many days, weeks, months, years, etc.

- *Depuis quand*

  Depuis quand habitez-vous cet appartement? / **Since when have you been living in this apartment?**

  J'habite cet appartement depuis le premier septembre. / **I have been living in this apartment since September first.**

  Note: When you use *depuis quand* in your question, you expect the other person to tell you since what particular point in time in the past — a particular day, date, month; in other words, since *when,* not *how long.*

  Depuis quand êtes-vous malade? / **Since when have you been sick?**

  Je suis malade depuis samedi. / **I have been sick since Saturday.**

  Depuis quand habitiez-vous l'appartement quand vous avez déménagé? / **Since when had you been living in the apartment when you moved?**

  J'habitais l'appartement depuis le cinq avril dernier quand j'ai déménagé. / **I had been living in the apartment since last April fifth, when I moved.**

Il y a + Length of Time + *que; voici* + Length of Time + *que; voilà* + Length of Time + *que*

- In Questions and Answers

  Depuis combien de temps attendez-vous l'autobus? / **How long have you been waiting for the bus?**

  J'attends l'autobus depuis vingt minutes. / **I have been waiting for the bus for twenty minutes.**

  Voici vingt minutes que je l'attends. / **I have been waiting for it for twenty minutes.**

  Voilà vingt minutes que je l'attends. / **I have been waiting for it for twenty minutes.**

  Note: When you use these expressions, you generally use them at the beginning of your answer + the verb.
  When you use the *depuis* construction, the verb comes first: *J'attends l'autobus depuis vingt minutes.*

- *Il y a* + length of time

  Il y a + length of time means "ago." Do not use *que* in this construction as in the above examples because the meaning is entirely different.

  Madame Martin est partie il y a une heure. / **Mrs. Martin left an hour ago.**

  L'autobus est arrivé il y a vingt minutes. / **The bus arrived twenty minutes ago.**

• *Il y a* and *Il y avait*

Il y a alone means "there is" or "there are" when you are merely making a statement.

> *Il y a vingt élèves dans cette classe.* / There are twenty students in this class.
> *Il y a une mouche dans la soupe.* / There is a fly in the soup.

Il y avait alone means "there was" or "there were" when you are merely making a statement.

> *Il y avait vingt élèves dans cette classe.* / There were (used to be) twenty students in this class.
> *Il y avait deux mouches dans la soupe.* / There were two flies in the soup.

Voici and *Voilà*

These two expressions are used to point out someone or something.

> *Voici un taxi!* / Here's a taxi!
> *Voilà un taxi là-bas!* / There's a taxi over there!
> *Voici ma carte d'identité et voilà mon passeport.* / Here's my ID card and there's my passport.
> *Voici mon père et voilà ma mère.* / Here's my father and there's my mother.

§12.2 BASIC EX-PRESSIONS

With *à*

à bicyclette / by bicycle, on a bicycle	*à haute voix* / aloud, out loud, in a loud voice
à bientôt / so long, see you soon	*à jamais* / forever
à cause de / on account of, because of	*à l'école* / at (in, to) school
à cette heure / at this time, at the present moment	*à l'étranger* / abroad, overseas
	à l'heure / on time
à cheval / on horseback	*à l'instant* / instantly
à côté de / beside, next to	*à l'occasion* / on the occasion
à demain / until tomorrow, see you tomorrow	*à la campagne* / at (in, to) the country(side)
à droite / at (on, to) the right	*à la fin* / at last, finally
	à la fois / at the same time
à gauche / at (on, to) the left	*à la main* / in one's hand, by hand
	à la maison / at home

à la mode / fashionable, in style, in fashion

à la radio / on the radio

à la recherche de / in search of

à la télé / on TV

à mon avis / in my opinion

à part / aside

à partir de / beginning with

à peine / hardly, scarcely

à peu près / approximately, about, nearly

à pied / on foot

à plus tard / see you later

à présent / now, at present

à propos / by the way

à propos de / about, with reference to, concerning

à quelle heure? / at what time?

à qui est ce livre? / whose is this book?

à quoi bon? / what's the use?

à son gré / to one's liking

à temps / in time

à tour de rôle / in turn

à tout à l'heure / see you in a little while

à tout prix / at any cost

à travers / across, through

à tue-tête / at the top of one's voice, as loud as possible

à vélo / on a bike

à voix basse / in a low voice, softly

à volonté / at will, willingly

à vrai dire / to tell the truth

à vue d'œil / visibly

With *au*

au bas de / at the bottom of

au besoin / if need be, if necessary

au bout de / at the end of, at the tip of

au contraire / on the contrary

au début / at (in) the beginning

au-dessous de / below, beneath

au-dessus de / above, over

au fond de / in the bottom of

au haut de / at the top of

au lieu de / instead of

au milieu de / in the middle of

au moins / at least

au pied de / at the foot of

au printemps / in the spring

au revoir / goodbye

au sous-sol / in the basement

au sujet de / about, concerning

au téléphone / on the telephone

café au lait / coffee with milk

rosbif au jus / roast beef with gravy

With *aux*

aux dépens / at the expense	*rire aux éclats* / to roar with laughter
aux pommes frites / with French fries	*sauter aux yeux* / to be evident, self-evident

With *aller*

aller / to feel (health): *Comment allez-vous?*	*aller à la rencontre de quelqu'un* / to go to meet someone
aller à / to be becoming, fit, suit: *Cette robe lui va bien.* / This dress suits her fine. *Sa barbe ne lui va pas.* / His beard does not look good on him.	*aller à pied* / to walk, go on foot
	aller au fond des choses / to get to the bottom of things
aller à la chasse / to go hunting	*aller chercher* / to go get
aller à la pêche / to go fishing	*allons donc!* / nonsense! come on, now!

With *avoir*

avoir . . . ans / to be . . . years old: *Quel âge — avez-vous?* / *J'ai dix-sept ans.*	*avoir besoin de* / to need, to have need of
avoir à + infinitive / to have to	*avoir bonne mine* / to look well
avoir affaire à quelqu'un / to deal with someone	*avoir chaud* / to be (feel) warm (persons)
avoir beau + infinitive / to be useless + infinitive, to do something in vain: *Vous avez beau parler; je ne vous écoute pas.* / You are talking in vain; I am not listening to you.	*avoir congé* / to have a day off, a holiday
	avoir de la chance / to be lucky
	avoir de quoi + infinitive / to have the material, means, enough + infinitive: *As-tu de quoi manger?* / Have you something (enough) to eat?

avoir des nouvelles / to receive news

avoir du savoir-faire / to have tact

avoir du savoir-vivre / to have good manners

avoir envie de + infinitive / to have a desire to

avoir faim / to be (feel) hungry

avoir froid / to be (feel) cold (persons)

avoir hâte / to be in a hurry

avoir honte / to be ashamed, to feel ashamed

avoir l'air + adjective / to seem, to look + adjective: *Vous avez l'air malade.* / You look sick.

avoir l'air de + infinitive / to appear + infinitive: *Vous avez l'air d'être malade.* / You appear to be sick.

avoir l'habitude de + infinitive / to be accustomed to, to be in the habit of: *J'ai l'habitude de faire mes devoirs avant le dîner.* / I'm in the habit of doing my homework before dinner.

avoir l'idée de + infinitive / to have a notion + infinitive

avoir l'intention de + infinitive / to intend + infinitive

avoir la bonté de + infinitive / to have the kindness

avoir la langue bien pendue / to have the gift of gab

avoir la parole / to have the floor (to speak)

avoir le cœur gros / to be heartbroken

avoir le temps de + infinitive / to have (the) time + infinitive

avoir lieu / to take place

avoir mal / to feel sick

avoir mal à + (place where it hurts) / to have a pain or ache in . . . : *J'ai mal à la jambe.* / My leg hurts. *J'ai mal au dos.* / My back hurts. *J'ai mal au cou.* / I have a pain in the neck.

avoir mauvaise mine / to look ill, not to look well

avoir peine à + infinitive / to have difficulty in + present participle

avoir peur de / to be afraid of

avoir pitié de / to take pity on

avoir raison / to be right (persons)

avoir soif / to be thirsty

avoir sommeil / to be sleepy

avoir son mot à dire / to have one's way

avoir tort / to be wrong (persons)

avoir une faim de loup / to be starving

With *bas*

au bas de / at the bottom of	*parler tout bas* / to speak very softly
en bas / downstairs, below	*de haut en bas* / from top to bottom
là-bas / over there	
A bas les devoirs! / Down with homework!	

With *bien*

bien des / many: *Roger a bien des amis.* / Roger has many friends.	*être bien aise* / to be very glad, happy
bien entendu / of course	*tant bien que mal* / rather badly, so-so
dire du bien de / to speak well of	

With *bon*

à quoi bon? / what's the use?	*de bon appétit* / with good appetite, heartily
bon gré, mal gré / willing or not, willy nilly	*de bon cœur* / gladly, willingly
bon marché / cheap, at a low price	*savoir bon gré à quelqu'un* / to be thankful, grateful to someone
bon pour quelqu'un / good to someone	

With *ça*

çà et là / here and there	*Ça va?* / Is everything okay?
Ça m'est égal. / It makes no difference to me.	*C'est comme ça!* / That's how it is!
comme ci, comme ça / so-so	*Pas de ça!* / None of that!

With *cela*

Cela est égal. / It's all the same. It doesn't matter. It makes no difference.	*Cela ne vous regarde pas.* / That's none of your business.
Cela m'est égal. / It doesn't matter to me. It's all the same to me.	*malgré cela* / in spite of that
	malgré tout cela / in spite of all that
Cela n'importe. / That doesn't matter.	*Qu'est-ce que cela veut dire?* / What does that mean?
Cela ne fait rien. / That makes no difference.	
Cela ne sert à rien. / That serves no purpose.	

With *ce, c'est, est-ce*

c'est-à-dire / that is, that is to say	*n'est-ce pas?* / isn't that so? isn't it?, etc.
C'est aujourd'hui lundi. / Today is Monday.	*Qu'est-ce que c'est?* / What is it?
C'est dommage. / It's a pity. It's too bad.	*Quel jour est-ce aujourd'hui?* / What day is it today? *C'est lundi.* / It's Monday.
C'est entendu. / It's understood. It's agreed. All right. OK.	
C'est épatant! / It's wonderful!	*Qu'est-ce qui s'est passé?* / What happened?
C'est trop fort! / That's just too much!	

With *d'*

comme d'habitude / as usual	*d'avance* / in advance, beforehand
d'abord / at first	*d'habitude* / ordinarily, usually, generally
d'accord / okay, agreed	
d'ailleurs / besides, moreover	*d'ici longtemps* / for a long time to come
d'aujourd'hui en huit / a week from today	*d'ordinaire* / ordinarily, usually, generally

changer d'avis / to change one's opinion, one's mind

tout d'un coup / all of a sudden

With de

au haut de / at the top of

autour de / around

changer de train / to change trains: changer de vêtements / to change clothes

combien de / how much, how many

de bon appétit / with good appetite, heartily

de bon cœur / gladly, willingly

de bonne heure / early

de cette façon / in this way

de jour en jour / from day to day

de l'autre côté de / on the other side of

de la part de / on behalf of, from

de nouveau / again

de parti pris / on purpose, deliberately

de plus / furthermore

de plus en plus / more and more

de quelle cou- leur . . . ? / what color . . . ?

de quoi + infinitive / something, enough + infinitive: de quoi écrire / something to write with; de quoi manger / something or enough to eat; de quoi vivre / something or enough to live on

de rien / you're welcome, don't mention it

de rigueur / required, obligatory

de son mieux / one's best

de suite / one after another, in succession

de temps en temps / from time to time, occasion- ally

de toutes ses forces / with all one's might, strenuously

du côté de / in the direction of, toward

éclater de rire / to burst out laughing

en face de / opposite

entendre parler de / to hear about

être de retour / to be back

être en train de / to be in the act of, in the process of

être temps de + infinitive / to be time + infinitive

faire semblant de + infinitive / to pretend + infinitive

féliciter quelqu'un de quelque chose / to congratulate someone for something

Il n'y a pas de quoi! / You're welcome!

jamais de la vie! / never in one's life! never! out of the question!

jouer de / to play (a musical instrument)

manquer de + infinitive / to fail to, to almost do something: *Victor a manqué de se noyer.* / Victor almost drowned.

mettre de côté / to lay aside, to save

pas de mal! / no harm!

près de / near

quelque chose de + adjective / something + adjective: *J'ai bu quelque chose de bon!* / I drank something good!

Quoi de neuf? / What's new?

Rien de neuf! / Nothing's new!

tout de même / all the same

tout de suite / immediately, at once

venir de + infinitive / to have just done something; *Je viens de manger.* / I have just eaten.

With *du*

dire du bien de quelqu'un / to speak well of someone

dire du mal de quelqu'un / to speak ill of someone

donner du chagrin à quelqu'un / to give someone grief

du côté de / in the direction of, toward

du matin au soir / from morning until night

du moins / at least

du reste / besides, in addition, furthermore

montrer du doigt / to point out, to show, to indicate by pointing

pas du tout / not at all

With *en*

de jour en jour / from day to day

de temps en temps / from time to time

en anglais, en français, etc. / in English, in French, etc.

en arrière / backwards, to the rear, behind

en automne, en hiver, en été / in the fall, in winter, in summer

en automobile / by car

en avion / by plane

en avoir plein le dos / to be sick and tired of something

en bas / downstairs, below

en bateau / by boat

en bois, en pierre, en + a material / made of wood, of stone, etc.

en chemin de fer / by train

en dessous (de) / underneath

en dessus (de) / above, on top, over

en effet / in fact, indeed, yes, indeed

en face de / opposite

en famille / as a family

en haut / upstairs, above

en huit jours / in a week

en même temps / at the same time

en panne / mechanical breakdown

en plein air / in the open air, outdoors

en retard / late, not on time

en tout cas / in any case, at any rate

en toute hâte / with all possible speed, haste

en ville / downtown, in (at, to) town

En voilà assez! / Enough of that!

en voiture / by car: en voiture! / all aboard!

être en train de + infinitive / to be in the act of + present participle, to be in the process of, to be busy + present participle

Je vous en prie. / I beg you. You're welcome.

mettre en pièces / to tear to pieces, to break into pieces

voir tout en rose / to see the bright side of things, to be optimistic

With être

être à l'heure / to be on time

être à quelqu'un / to belong to someone: Ce livre est à moi. / This book belongs to me.

être au courant de / to be informed about

être bien / to be comfortable

être d'accord avec / to agree with

être de retour / to be back

être en retard / to be late, not to be on time

être en train de + infinitive / to be in the act of, to be in the process of, to be busy + present participle

être en vacances / to be on vacation

être enrhumé / to have a cold, be sick with a cold

être pressé(e) / to be in a hurry

Quelle heure est-il? /What time is it? Il est une heure. / It is one o'clock. Il est deux heures. / It is two o'clock

With *faire*

Cela ne fait rien. / That doesn't matter.
Comment se fait-il? / How come?

faire à sa tête / to have one's way
faire attention (à) / to pay attention (to)
faire beau / to be pleasant, nice weather
faire bon accueil / to welcome
faire chaud / to be warm (weather)
faire de l'autostop / to hitchhike
faire de son mieux / to do one's best
faire des châteaux en Espagne / to build castles in the air
faire des emplettes; faire des courses; faire du shopping / to do or to go shopping
faire des progrès / to make progress
faire du bien à quelqu'un / to do good for someone
faire du vélo / to ride a bike
faire exprès / to do on purpose
faire face à / to oppose
faire froid / to be cold (weather)
faire jour / to be daylight
faire la bête / to act like a fool

faire la connaissance de quelqu'un / to make the acquaintance of someone, meet someone for the first time
faire la cuisine / to do the cooking
faire la grasse matinée / to sleep late in the morning
faire la lessive / to do the laundry
faire (une) la malle / to pack (a) the trunk
faire la queue / to line up, to get in line, to stand in line
faire la vaisselle / to do (wash) the dishes
faire le ménage / to do housework
faire les bagages / to pack the baggage, luggage
faire les valises / to pack the suitcases, valises
faire mal à quelqu'un / to hurt, to harm someone
faire nuit / to be night(time)
faire peur à quelqu'un / to frighten someone
faire plaisir à quelqu'un / to please someone
faire sa toilette / to wash and dress oneself
faire ses adieux / to say goodbye
faire son possible / to do one's best
faire suivre le courrier / to forward mail

faire un tour / to go for a stroll

faire un voyage / to take a trip

faire une partie de / to play a game of

faire une promenade / to take a walk

faire une visite / to pay a visit

faire venir quelqu'un / to have someone come: *Il a fait venir le docteur.* / He had the doctor come.

faire venir l'eau à la bouche / to make one's mouth water

Faites comme chez vous! / Make yourself at home!

Que faire? / What is to be done?

Quel temps fait-il? / What's the weather like?

With *mieux*

aimer mieux / to prefer, like better

aller mieux / to feel better (person's health): *Êtes-vous toujours malade?* / Are you still sick? *Je vais mieux, merci.* / I'm feeling better, thank you.

de son mieux / one's best

faire de son mieux / to do one's best

tant mieux / so much the better

valoir mieux / to be better (worth more), to be preferable

With *non*

Je crois que non. / I don't think so.

Mais non! / Of course not!

Non merci! / No, thank you!

J'espère bien que non. / I hope not.

With *par*

par bonheur / fortunately

par-ci; par-là / here and there

par conséquent / consequently, therefore

par exemple / for example

par hasard / by chance

par ici / through here, this way, in this direction

par jour / per day, daily

par la fenêtre / out, through the window

par-là / through there, that way, in that direction

par malheur / unfortunately

par mois / per month, monthly

par semaine / per week, weekly

par tous les temps / in all kinds of weather

apprendre par cœur / to learn by heart, memorize

finir par + infinitive / to end up + present participle: *Ils ont fini par se marier.* / They ended up by getting married.

jeter l'argent par la fenêtre / to waste money

With *plus*

de plus / furthermore, besides, in addition

de plus en plus / more and more

n'en pouvoir plus / to be exhausted, not to be able to go on any longer: *Je n'en peux plus!* / I can't go on any longer!

Plus ça change plus c'est la même chose. / The more it changes, the more it remains the same.

une fois de plus / once more, one more time

With *quel*

Quel âge avez-vous? / How old are you?

Quel garçon! / What a boy!

Quel jour est-ce aujourd'hui? / What day is it today?

With *quelle*

De quelle couleur est (sont) . . . ? / What color is (are) . . . ?

Quelle fille! / What a girl!

Quelle heure est-il? / What time is it?

Quelle chance! / What luck!

With *quelque chose*

quelque chose à + infinitive / something + infinitive: *J'ai quelque chose à lui dire.* / I have something to say to him (to her).	*quelque chose de* + adjective / something + adjective: *J'ai quelque chose d'intéressant à vous dire.* / I have something interesting to tell you.

With *quoi*

à quoi bon? / what's the use? *avoir de quoi* + infinitive / to have something (enough) + infinitive: *Avez-vous de quoi écrire?* / Do you have something to write with?	*avoir de quoi manger* / to have something to eat *Il n'y a pas de quoi!* / You're welcome! *Quoi de neuf?* / What's new?

With *rien*

Cela ne fait rien. / That doesn't matter. *Cela ne sert à rien.* / That serves no purpose.	*de rien* / you're welcome, don't mention it *Rien de neuf!* / Nothing's new!

With *tant*

tant bien que mal / so-so *tant mieux* / so much the better *tant pis* / so much the worse *J'ai tant de travail!* / I have so much work!	*Je t'aime tant!* / I love you so much! *tant de choses* / so many things

With *tous*

tous (les) deux / both (m. plural)	*tous les soirs* / every evening
tous les ans / every year	*tous les mois* / every month
tous les jours / every day	
tous les matins / every morning	

With *tout*

après tout / after all	*tout d'un coup* / all of a sudden
en tout cas / in any case, at any rate	*tout de même!* / all the same! just the same!
pas du tout / not at all	*tout de suite* / immediately, at once, right away
tout à coup / suddenly	
tout à fait / completely, entirely	
tout à l'heure / a little while ago, in a little while	*tout le monde* / everybody
tout d'abord / first of all	*tout le temps* / all the time

With *toute*

en toute hâte / with all possible speed, in great haste	*toutes (les) deux* / both (f. plural)
toute chose / everything	*toutes les nuits* / every night
de toutes ses forces / with all one's might	

With *y*

il y a + length of time / ago: *il y a un mois* / a month ago	*Il n'y a pas de quoi.* / You're welcome.
il y a / there is, there are	*y compris* / including
il y avait . . . / there was (there were) . . .	

§13.

Dates, Days, Months, Seasons

§13.1

Dates

Quelle est la date aujourd'hui? / What's the date today?
Quel jour sommes-nous aujourd'hui? / What's the date today?

C'est aujourd'hui le premier octobre. / Today is October first.
C'est aujourd'hui le deux novembre. / Today is November second.

C'est lundi. / It's Monday.
C'est aujourd'hui mardi. / Today is Tuesday.

Quand êtes-vous né(e)? / When were you born?
Je suis né(e) le vingt-deux août, mil neuf cent soixante-six. / I was born on August 22, 1966.

Use the cardinal numbers for dates, except "the first," which is *le premier.*

§13.2

Days

The days of the week, which are all masculine, are:

dimanche / Sunday   *jeudi* / Thursday
lundi / Monday   *vendredi* / Friday
mardi / Tuesday   *samedi* / Saturday
mercredi / Wednesday

§13.3

Months

The months of the year, which are all masculine, are:

janvier / January   *juillet* / July
février / February   *août* / August
mars / March   *septembre* / September
avril / April   *octobre* / October
mai / May   *novembre* / November
juin / June   *décembre* / December

To say "in" + the name of the month, use *en: en janvier, en février;* OR *au mois de janvier, au mois de février* / in the month of January, etc.

§13.4

Seasons

The seasons of the year, which are all masculine, are:

le printemps / spring   *l'automne* / fall
l'été / summer   *l'hiver* / winter

| Mnemonic tip | *En hiver,* you shiver.

To say "in" + the name of the season, use *en* except with *printemps: au printemps, en été, en automne, en hiver* / in spring, in summer, etc.

§14.

Telling Time

Il est une heure et demie.

Quelle heure est-il? / What time is it?
Il est une heure. / It is one o'clock.
Il est une heure dix. / It is ten minutes after one.
Il est une heure et quart. / It is a quarter after one.
Il est deux heures et demie. / It is half past two; it is two thirty.
Il est trois heures moins vingt. / It is twenty minutes to three.
Il est trois heures moins le quart. / It is a quarter to three.
Il est midi. / It is noon.
Il est minuit. / It is midnight.
à quelle heure? / at what time?
à une heure / at one o'clock
à une heure précise / at exactly one o'clock
à deux heures précises / at exactly two o'clock
à neuf heures du matin / at nine in the morning
à trois heures de l'après-midi / at three in the afternoon
à dix heures du soir / at ten in the evening
à l'heure / on time
à temps / in time
vers trois heures / around three o'clock; about three o'clock
un quart d'heure / a quarter of an hour; a quarter hour
une demi-heure / a half hour
Il est midi et demi / It is twelve thirty; It is half past twelve (noon).
Il est minuit et demi. / It is twelve thirty; It is half past twelve (midnight).

- In telling time, *Il est* + the hour is used, whether it is one or more than one, e.g., *Il est une heure. Il est deux heures.*

- If the time is after the hour, state the hour, then the minutes: *Il est une heure dix.*

- The conjunction *et* is used with *quart* after the hour and with *demi* or *demie: Il est une heure et quart. Il est une heure et demie. Il est midi et demi.*

139

The masculine form *demi* is used after a masculine noun: *Il est midi et demi.* The feminine form *demie* is used after a feminine noun: *Il est deux heures et demie.*

Demi remains *demi* when before a feminine or masculine noun, and is joined to the noun with a hyphen: *une demi-heure.*

• If the time expressed is before the hour, *moins* is used: *Il est trois heures moins vingt.*

• A quarter after the hour is *et quart;* a quarter to the hour is *moins le quart.*

• To express A.M. use *du matin;* to express P.M. use *de l'après-midi* if the time is in the afternoon; *du soir* if in the evening.

§14.2 "OFFICIAL" TIME EXPRESSIONS

Another way to tell time is the official time used by the French government on radio and TV, in railroad and bus stations, and at airports.

• It is the twenty-four-hour system.

• In this system, *quart, demi, demie, moins,* and *et* are not used.

• When you hear or see the stated time, subtract twelve from the number you hear or see. If the number is less than twelve, it is A.M. time, except for *24 heures,* which is midnight; *zéro heure* is also midnight.

EXAMPLES

> *Il est treize heures.* / It is 1:00 P.M.
> *Il est quinze heures.* / It is 3:00 P.M.
> *Il est vingt heures trente.* / It is 8:30 P.M.
> *Il est minuit.* / It is midnight.
> *It est seize heures trente.* / It is 4:30 P.M.
> *Il est dix-huit heures quinze.* / It is 6:15 P.M.
> *Il est vingt heures quarante-cinq.* / It is 8:45 P.M.
> *Il est vingt-deux heures cinquante.* / It is 10:50 P.M.

The abbreviation for *heure* or *heures* is *h.*

EXAMPLES

> *Il est 20 h. 20.* / It is 8:20 P.M.
> *Il est 15 h. 50.* / It is 3:50 P.M.
> *Il est 23 h. 30.* / It is 11:30 P.M.

§15.

Talking About the Weather

Quel temps fait -il? / What's the weather like?

WITH *Il fait . . .*

Il fait beau. / The weather is fine. The weather is beautiful.
Il fait beau temps. / The weather is beautiful.
Il fait chaud. / It's warm.
Il fait clair. / It is clear.
Il fait doux. / It's mild.
Il fait du soleil. / It's sunny. (You can also say *Il fait soleil.*)
Il fait du tonnerre. / It's thundering. (OR: *Il tonne.*)
Il fait du vent. / It's windy.
Il fait frais. / It is cool.
Il fait froid. / It's cold.
Il fait humide. / It's humid.
Il fait mauvais. / The weather is bad.

WITH *Il fait un temps . . .*

Il fait un temps affreux. / The weather is frightful.
Il fait un temps calme. / The weather is calm.
Il fait un temps couvert. / The weather is cloudy.
Il fait un temps lourd. / It's muggy.
Il fait un temps magnifique. / The weather is magnificent.
Il fait un temps superbe. / The weather is superb.

WITH *Le temps* + **VERB . . .**

Le temps menace. / The weather is threatening.
Le temps se gâte. / The weather is getting bad.
Le temps se met au beau. / The weather is getting beautiful.
Le temps se met au froid. / It's getting cold.
Le temps se rafraîchit. / The weather is getting cool.

WITH *Le ciel est . . .*

Le ciel est bleu. / The sky is blue.
Le ciel est calme. / The sky is calm.
Le ciel est couvert. / The sky is cloudy.
Le ciel est gris. / The sky is gray.

WITH OTHER VERBS

Il gèle. / It's freezing.
Il grêle. / It's hailing.
Il neige. / It's snowing.
Il pleut. / It's raining.
Il tombe de la grêle. / It's hailing.

§16.

Numbers

Cardinal Numbers: 1 to 1000

0 *zéro* 1 *un, une* 2 *deux* 3 *trois* 4 *quatre* 5 *cinq* 6 *six* 7 *sept* 8 *huit* 9 *neuf* 10 *dix* 11 *onze* 12 *douze* 13 *treize* 14 *quatorze* 15 *quinze* 16 *seize* 17 *dix-sept* 18 *dix-huit* 19 *dix-neuf*	70 *soixante-dix* 71 *soixante et onze* 72 *soixante-douze*, etc.
	80 *quatre-vingts* 81 *quatre-vingt-un* 82 *quatre-vingt-deux*, etc.
	90 *quatre-vingt-dix* 91 *quatre-vingt-onze* 92 *quatre-vingt-douze*, etc.
	100 *cent* 101 *cent un* 102 *cent deux*, etc.
	200 *deux cents* 201 *deux cent un* 202 *deux cent deux*, etc.
20 *vingt* 21 *vingt et un* 22 *vingt-deux*, etc.	300 *trois cents* 301 *trois cent un* 302 *trois cent deux*, etc.
30 *trente* 31 *trente et un* 32 *trente-deux*, etc.	400 *quatre cents* 401 *quatre cent un* 402 *quatre cent deux*, etc.
40 *quarante* 41 *quarante et un* 42 *quarante-deux*, etc.	500 *cinq cents* 501 *cinq cent un* 502 *cinq cent deux*, etc.
50 *cinquante* 51 *cinquante et un* 52 *cinquante-deux*, etc.	600 *six cents* 601 *six cent un* 602 *six cent deux*, etc.
60 *soixante* 61 *soixante et un* 62 *soixante-deux*, etc.	700 *sept cents* 701 *sept cent un* 702 *sept cent deux*, etc.

800 *huit cents* 801 *huit cent un* 802 *huit cent deux*, etc.	**Mnemonic tip** If you're not sure that *vingt* is spelled with *ng* or *gn*, note this: V I N G T T W E N T Y
900 *neuf cents* 901 *neuf cent un* 902 *neuf cent deux*, etc.	
1000 *mille*	

Mnemonic tip Pronounce *seize* (16) as in English "**Says who?**"

Simple Arithmetical Expressions

deux et deux font quatre	$2 + 2 = 4$
trois fois cinq font quinze	$3 \times 5 = 15$
douze moins dix font deux	$12 - 10 = 2$
dix divisés par deux font cinq	$10 \div 2 = 5$

Fractions

½	*un demi*	a (one) half
⅓	*un tiers*	a (one) third
¼	*un quart*	a (one) fourth
⅕	*un cinquième*	a (one) fifth

Approximate Amounts

une dizaine	about ten
une quinzaine	about fifteen
une vingtaine	about twenty
une trentaine	about thirty
une quarantaine	about forty
une cinquantaine	about fifty
une soixantaine	about sixty
une centaine	about a hundred
un millier	about a thousand

Mnemonic tip You can remember that *une quarantaine* is about 40 because there are 40 days in a "quarantine."

Ordinal Numbers: First to Twentieth

first	premier, première	1st	1er, 1re
second	deuxième (second, seconde)	2d	2^e
third	troisième	3d	3^e
fourth	quatrième	4th	4^e
fifth	cinquième	5th	5^e
sixth	sixième	6th	6^e
seventh	septième	7th	7^e
eighth	huitième	8th	8^e
ninth	neuvième	9th	9^e
tenth	dixième	10th	10^e
eleventh	onzième	11th	11^e
twelfth	douzième	12th	12^e
thirteenth	treizième	13th	13^e
fourteenth	quatorzième	14th	14^e
fifteenth	quinzième	15th	15^e
sixteenth	seizième	16th	16^e
seventeenth	dix-septième	17th	17^e
eighteenth	dix-huitième	18th	18^e
nineteenth	dix-neuvième	19th	19^e
twentieth	vingtième	20th	20^e

Some observations:

• You must learn the difference between cardinal and ordinal numbers. If you have trouble distinguishing between the two, just remember that we use cardinal numbers most of the time: *un, deux, trois* (one, two, three), and so on.

• Use ordinal numbers to express a certain order: *premier* (*première,* if the noun following is feminine), *deuxième, troisième* (first, second, third), and so on.

• *Premier* is the masculine singular form and *première* is the feminine singular form. Examples: *le premier homme* / the first man, *la première femme* / the first woman.

• The masculine singular form *second,* or the feminine singular form *seconde,* is used to mean "second" when there are only two. When there are more than two, *deuxième* is used: *le Second Empire,* because there were only two empires in France, but *la Deuxième République,* because there have been more than two republics in France.

• The raised letters in *1er* are the last two letters in the word *premier;* it is equivalent to our "st" in 1st. The raised letters in *1ʳᵉ* are the last two letters in the word *première,* which is the feminine singular form of "first."

The raised letter *e* after an ordinal number (for example, *2ᵉ*) stands for the *-ième* ending of a French ordinal number.

- When referring to sovereigns or rulers, the only ordinal number used is *premier.* For all other designations, the cardinal numbers are used. The definite article "the" is used in English but not in French. Examples:

François 1ᵉʳ	*François Premier*	Francis the First
	BUT	
Louis XIV	*Louis Quatorze*	Louis the Fourteenth

§17.

Synonyms (similar meanings)

aide n.f., *secours* n.m.	aid, help
aimer mieux v., *préférer*	to like better, prefer
aliment n.m., *nourriture* n.f.	food, nourishment
anneau n.m., *bague* n.f.	ring (on finger)
arriver v., *se passer*	to happen, occur
aussitôt que conj., *dès que*	as soon as
auteur n.m. *écrivain* n.m.	author, writer
bâtiment n.m., *édifice*, n.m.	building, edifice
bâtir v., *construire*	to build, construct
beaucoup de adv., *bien des*	many
bref. brève adj., *court, courte*	brief, short
casser v., *rompre, briser*	to break
causer v., *parler*	to chat, talk
centre n.m., *milieu,* n.m.	center, middle
certain (certaine) adj., *sûr, sûre*	certain, sure
cesser v., *arrêter*	to cease, to stop
chagrin n.m., *souci* n.m.	sorrow, trouble, care, concern
chemin n.m., *route* n.f.	road, route
commencer à + infinitive, v., *se mettre à* + infinitive	to commence, begin, start
conseil n.m., *avis* n.m.	counsel, advice, opinion
content, (contente) adj., *heureux (heureuse)*	content, happy
de façon que conj., *de manière que*	so that, in such a way
décéder v., *mourir*	to die
dégoût n.m., *répugnance* n.f.	disgust, repugnance
dérober v., *voler*	to rob, steal
désirer v., *vouloir*	to desire, want
disputer v., *contester*	to dispute, argue, contest
docteur n.m., *médecin,* n.m.	doctor, physician
embrasser v., *donner un baiser*	to embrace, hug; to give a kiss
employer v., *se servir de*	to employ, use, make use of
épouvanter v., *effrayer*	to frighten, terrify, scare
erreur n.f., *faute,* n.f.	error, fault, mistake
espèce n.f., *sorte,* n.f.	species, type, kind, sort

adj.: adjective; adv.: adverb; conj.: conjunction; f.: feminine; m.: masculine; n.: noun; prep.: preposition; v.: verb

essayer de + infinitive, v., *tâcher de* + infinitive	to try, to attempt + infinitive
étrennes n.f., *cadeau* n.m.	Christmas gifts, present, gift
façon n.f., *manière,* n.f.	way, manner
fameux, (fameuse) adj., *célèbre*	famous, celebrated
fatigué, (fatiguée) adj., *épuisé, (épuisée)*	tired, fatigued, exhausted
favori, (favorite) adj., *préféré (préférée)*	favorite, preferred
fin n.f., *bout* n.m.	end
finir v., *terminer*	to finish, end, terminate
frémir v., *trembler*	to shiver, quiver, tremble
galette n.f., *gâteau* n.m.	cake
gaspiller v., *dissiper*	to waste, dissipate
gâter v., *abîmer*	to spoil, ruin, damage
glace n.f., *miroir* n.m.	hand mirror, mirror
grossier, grossière adj., *vulgaire*	gross, vulgar, cheap, common
habiter v., *demeurer*	to live (in), dwell, inhabit
haïr v., *détester*	to hate, detest
image n.f., *tableau* n.m.	image, picture
indiquer v., *montrer*	to indicate, show
jadis adv., *autrefois*	formerly, in times gone by
jeu n.m., *divertissement,* n.m.	game, amusement
labourer v, *travailler*	to labor, work
laisser v., *permettre*	to allow, permit
lier v., *attacher*	to tie, attach
lieu n.m., *endroit,* n.m.	place, spot, location
logis n.m. *habitation* n.f.	lodging, dwelling
lutter v., *combattre*	to struggle, fight, combat
maître n.m. *instituteur,* n.m.	master, teacher, instructor
maîtresse n.f. *institutrice,* n.f.	mistress, teacher, instructor
mauvais (mauvaise) adj., *méchant (méchante)*	bad, mean, nasty
mener v., *conduire*	to lead; to take (someone)
mince adj., *grêle*	thin, slender, skinny
naïf (naïve) adj., *ingénu (ingénue)*	naive, simple, innocent
net (nette) adj., *propre*	neat, clean
noces n.f., *mariage* n.m.	wedding, marriage
œuvre n.f., *travail* n.m.	work
ombre n.f., *obscurité* n.f.	shade, shadow, darkness
ombrelle n.f., *parasol* n.m.	sunshade, parasol, beach umbrella

parce que conj., *car*	because, for
pareil (pareille) adj., *égal (égale)*	similar, equivalent, equal
parvenir à v., *réussir à*	to succeed, to attain
pays n.m., *nation* n.f.	country, nation
pensée n.f., *idée,* n.f.	thought, idea
penser v., *réfléchir*	to think, reflect
penser à v., *songer à*	to think of; to dream of
professeur n.m., *maître,* n.m., *maîtresse,* n.f.	professor, teacher
puis adv., *ensuite*	then, afterwards
quand conj., *lorsque*	when
quelquefois adv., *parfois*	sometimes, at times
se rappeler v., *se souvenir de*	to recall, to remember
rester v., *demeurer*	to stay, to remain
sérieux (sérieuse) adj., *grave*	serious, grave
seulement adv., *ne* + verb + *que*	only
soin n.m., *attention* n.f.	care, attention
soulier n.m., *chaussure* n.f.	shoe, footwear
tout de suite adv., *immédi- atement*	right away, immediately
triste adj., *malheureux (malheureuse)*	sad, unhappy
vêtements n.m., *habits,* n.m.	clothes, clothing
visage n.m., *figure* n.f.	face
vite adv., *rapidement*	quickly, rapidly

Mnemonic tip	*Bref* is brief and *court* is short because it contains the English word "curt" (brief, short).

Mnemonic tip	*Une chaussure* is a shoe because it contains *sur* / on, and you put it on your foot.

Mnemonic tip	*Une chaussette* is a sock because it's something like an anklet(te) sock.

Mnemonic tip	*Une parole* is a spoken word because when a prisoner is on *"parole"* he gives his word that he will behave in a civil manner.

Mnemonic tip	When you give someone *conseil,* you give him counsel, advice.

Mnemonic tip	When you *embrasser* a person, you put your *bras* / arms around that person.

§18.

Antonyms (opposites)

absent (absente) adj, absent	*présent (présente)* adj., present
acheter v., to buy	*vendre* v., to sell
agréable adj., pleasant, agreeable	*désagréable* adj., unpleasant, disagreeable
aimable adj., kind	*méchant (méchante)* adj., mean, nasty
aller v., to go	*venir* v., to come
ami (amie) n., friend	*ennemi (ennemie)* n., enemy
s'amuser refl. v., to enjoy oneself, to have a good time	*s'ennuyer* refl. v., to be bored
ancien (ancienne) adj., old, ancient	*nouveau (nouvel, nouvelle)* adj., new
avant prep., before	*après* prep., after
bas (basse) adj., low	*haut (haute)* adj., high
beau (bel, belle) adj., beautiful, handsome	*laid (laide)* adj., ugly
beaucoup (de) adv., much, many	*peu (de)* adv., little, some
beauté n.f., beauty	*laideur* n.f., ugliness
bête adj., stupid	*intelligent (intelligente)* adj., intelligent
bon (bonne) adj., good	*mauvais (mauvaise)* adj., bad
bonheur n.m., happiness	*malheur* n.m., unhappiness
chaud (chaude) adj., hot, warm	*froid (froide)* adj., cold
cher (chère) adj., expensive	*bon marché* cheap
content (contente) adj., glad, pleased	*mécontent (mécontente)* adj., displeased
court (courte) adj., short	*long (longue)* adj., long
debout adv., standing	*assis (assise)* adj., seated, sitting
dedans adv., inside	*dehors* adv., outside
demander v., to ask	*répondre* v., to reply
dernier (dernière) adj., last	*premier (première)* adj., first
derrière adv., prep., behind, in back of	*devant* adv., prep., in front of
dessous adv., prep., below, underneath	*dessus* adv., prep., above, over
différent (différente) adj., different	*pareil (pareille)* adj., same, similar

adj.: adjective; adv.: adverb; conj.: conjunction; f.: feminine; m.: masculine; n.: noun; prep.: preposition; v.: verb

difficile adj., difficult
domestique adj., domestic
donner v., to give
droite n.f., right

emprunter v., to borrow
entrer (dans) v., to enter (in, into)
est n.m., east
étroit (étroite) adj., narrow

faible adj., weak
fermer v., to close
fin n.f., end

finir v., to finish

gagner v., to win
gai (gaie) adj., gay, happy
grand (grande) adj., large, tall, big
gros (grosse) adj., fat
grossier (grossière) adj., coarse, impolite

heureux (heureuse) adj., happy

ici adv., here
inutile adj., useless

jamais adv., never
jeune adj., young
jeunesse n.f., youth
joli (jolie) adj., pretty
jour n.m., day

léger (légère) adj., light
lentement adv., slowly

mal adv., badly
moderne adj., modern

moins adv., less
monter v., to go up
mourir v., to die
né (née) adj., past part., born

nord n.m., north
nouveau (nouvel, nouvelle) adj., new

facile adj., easy
sauvage adj., wild
recevoir v., to receive
gauche n.f., left

prêter v., to lend
sortir (de) v., to go out (of, from)
ouest n.m., west
large adj., wide

fort (forte) adj., strong
ouvrir v., to open
commencement n.m., beginning
commencer v., to begin; *se mettre à* v., to begin + inf.

perdre v., to lose
triste adj., sad
petit (petite) adj., small, little

maigre adj., thin
poli (polie) adj., polite

malheureux (malheureuse) adj., unhappy
là-bas adv., there
utile adj., useful

toujours adv., always
vieux (vieil, vieille) adj., old
vieillesse n.f., old age
laid (laide) adj., ugly
nuit n.f., night

lourd (lourde) adj., heavy
vite adv., quickly

bien adv., well
ancien (ancienne) adj., ancient, old

plus adv., more
descendre v., to go down
naître v., to be born
mort (morte) adj., past part., died, dead

sud n.m., south
vieux (vieil, vieille) adj., old

obéir (à) v., to obey

désobéir (à) v., to disobey

ôter v., to remove, to take off

mettre v., to put, to put on

oui adv., yes

non adv., no

paix n.f., peace

guerre n.f., war

paraître v., to appear

disparaître v., to disappear

paresseux (paresseuse) adj., lazy

travailleur (travailleuse) adj., diligent

partir v., to leave

arriver v., to arrive

pauvre adj., poor

riche adj., rich

perdre v., to lose

trouver v., to find

plancher n.m., floor

plafond n.m., ceiling

plein (pleine) adj., full

vide adj., empty

poli (polie) adj., polite

impoli (impolie) adj., impolite

possible adj., possible

impossible adj., impossible

prendre v., to take

donner v., to give

près (de) adv., prep., near

loin (de) adv., prep., far (from)

propre adj., clean

sale adj., dirty

quelque chose pron., something

rien pron., nothing

quelqu'un pron., someone, somebody

personne pron., nobody, no one

question n.f., question

réponse n.f., answer, reply, response

refuser v., to refuse

accepter v., to accept

réussir (à) v., to succeed (at, in)

échouer (à) v., to fail (at, in)

rire v., to laugh

pleurer v., to cry, to weep

sans prep., without

avec prep., with

silence n.m., silence

bruit n.m., noise

souvent adv., often

rarement adv., rarely

sur prep., on

sous prep., under

sûr (sûre) adj., sure, certain

incertain (incertaine) adj., unsure, uncertain

tôt adv., early

tard adv., late

travailler v., to work

jouer v., to play

travailleur (travailleuse) adj., diligent, hardworking

paresseux (paresseuse) adj., lazy

vie n.f., life

mort n.f., death

vivre v., to live

mourir v., to die

vrai (vraie) adj., true

faux (fausse) adj., false

| Mnemonic tip | The verb *mourir* (to die) has one *r* because a person dies once; *nourrir* (to nourish) has two *r*'s because a person is nourished more than once. |

| Mnemonic tip | The word *dessous* (below, underneath) contains *sous* (under). |

| Mnemonic tip | The word *dessus* (above, over) contains *sus,* which reminds you of *sur* (on). |

| Mnemonic tip | *Perdre* means "to lose" because perdition is a place for lost souls. |

| Mnemonic tip | Detroit, a city in Michigan, is on the Detroit River, which is narrow *(étroit)* in spots. |

| Mnemonic tip | A floor *(le plancher)* was originally made of wooden planks. |

| Mnemonic tip | Pronounce *bonne* as in the English word "bun." |

| Mnemonic tip | You "mount" a mountain when you *monter une montagne.* |

| Mnemonic tip | You go **a**way when you *p**a**rtir* and you go **o**ut when you *s**o**rtir. Partir* and "**a**way" contain **a**'s. *Sortir* and "g**o** **o**ut" contain **o**'s. |

| Mnemonic tip | If you don't know your right from your left, *droite* contains "it" and so does "right." |

§19.

Cognates

In addition to studying synonyms in §17. and antonyms in §18., another good way to increase your vocabulary is to become aware of cognates. A *cognate* is a word whose origin is the same as another word in another language. There are many cognates in French and English whose spelling is sometimes identical or very similar. Most of the time, the meaning is the same or similar; sometimes they appear to be related because of similar spelling, but they are not true cognates. You will find a list of these "false cognates" or "tricky words" in §20.

Generally speaking, certain endings, or suffixes, of French words have English equivalents.

EXAMPLES

French Suffix	Equivalent English Suffix	French Word	English Word
-able	-able	adorable aimable	adorable amiable (likeable)
-aire	-ary	le dictionnaire	dictionary
-eux -euse	-ous	fameux fameuse	famous
-ieux -ieuse	-ous	gracieux gracieuse	gracious
-iste	-ist	le (la) dentiste	dentist
-ité	-ity	la qualité	quality
-ment	-ly	correctement	correctly
-mettre	-mit	admettre	admit
-oire	-ory	la mémoire	memory
-phie	-phy	la photographie	photography
-scrire	-scribe	transcrire	transcribe

A French word that contains the circumflex accent (^) over a vowel means that there used to be an *s* right after that vowel.

EXAMPLES

hâte / haste	hôtel / hostel	bête / beast	île / isle
pâte / paste	honnête / honest	fête / feast	vêpres / vespers
bâtard / bastard	plâtre / plaster	mât / mast	prêtre / priest

But you don't always get a cognate if you insert an *s* right after the vowel that contains a circumflex.

EXAMPLES

gâteau / cake   *bêler* / to bleat   *bâtiment* / building   *âme* / soul

Mnemonic tip | If you confuse *le gâteau* (cake) with *le bateau* (boat) because you can't remember which one contains the circumflex accent, remember that the ˆ in *gâteau* is the icing on top of the cake!

§20.

Tricky Words

"False friends" are look-alikes but have different meanings.

actualités n.f., pl. news reports
actuel adj. present, present-day
actuellement adv. at present
addition n.f. bill (check)
attendre v. to wait

belle adj., fem. beautiful
bénir v. to bless
blesser v. to wound
bras n.m. arm
but n.m. goal

cabinet n.m. office; study
car conj. because
causer v. to chat; to cause
cave n.f. cellar, basement
chair n.f. flesh
chat n.m. cat
chose n.f. thing
coin n.m. corner
comment adv. how
conférence n.f. lecture
crâne n.m. skull
crayon n.m. pencil

dent n.f. tooth
dire v. to say, to tell
dot n.f. dowry

éditeur n.m. publisher
essence n.f. gasoline

fin n.f. end
flèche n.f. arrow
fort adj., n. strong
four n.m. oven
front n.m. forehead

grand adj., m. tall, big, large
grave adj. serious

haïr v. to hate

journal n.m. newspaper

large adj. wide, broad
lecture n.f. reading
librairie n.f. bookstore

magasin n.m. store
main n.f. hand
marine n.f. navy; seascape
médecin n.m. doctor, physician
médecine n.f. medicine (study of)
médicament n.m. medicine
mine n.f. facial appearance
monnaie n.f. change (coins)

on pers. pron. one, someone, they
ours n.m. bear (animal)

pain n.m. bread
pal n.m. pale, stake (for punishment)
par prep. by
personnel adj. personal
pie n.f. magpie (bird)
pile n.f. battery; pile, heap
place n.f. plaza, place
plate adj., fem. flat
pour prep. for
prune n.f. plum
pruneau n.m. prune

raisin n.m. grape
raisin sec n.m. raisin
râpe n.f. grater (cheese)
rose adj. pink
rose n. rose
rue n.f. street

sable n.m. sand
sale adj. dirty, soiled
sensible adj. sensitive
son n.m. sound

stage n.m. training course of study

stylo n.m. pen

tôt adv. early

vent n.m. wind (air)

vie n.f. life

LET'S REVIEW

Test Yourself

§1. PRONOUNCING FRENCH SOUNDS

Choose the correct answer by circling the letter.

1. The vowel *a* in the French word *la* is pronounced as in the English word
   A. at   B. ate   C. father   D. ago

2. The vowel *a* in the French word *pas* is pronounced as in the English word
   A. father   B. at   C. ate   D. bare

3. The vowel *é* in the French word *thé* is pronounced as in the English word
   A. ate   B. less   C. week   D. the

4. The vowel *i* in the French word *ici* is pronounced as in the English word
   A. see   B. it   C. idea   D. lie

5. The semiconsonant sound in the French word *oui* is pronounced as in the English word
   A. week   B. ouch   C. pooch   D. pouch

6. The consonant *ç* in the French word *ça* is pronounced as in the English word
   A. sorry   B. cat   C. pack   D. church

7. The vowel *è* in the French word *père* is pronounced as in the English word
   A. egg   B. week   C. the   D. say

8. The vowel *e* in the French word *le* is pronounced as in the English word
   A. ago   B. less   C. weak   D. lay

9. The sound of *ch* in the French word *chose* is pronounced as in the English word
   A. choose   B. chair   C. share   D. character

10. The sound of *u* in the French word *tu* is pronounced as in the English word
    A. tuck   B. push   C. much   D. cute

§2.
CAPITALIZA-
TION, PUNC-
TUATION
MARKS,
WORD
DIVISION

I. Divide the following French words into syllables.

EXAMPLE: *beaucoup*   *beau / coup*

1. *école* ____   2. *important* ____   3. *après* ____

II. Match the French words for punctuation marks with their English equivalents.

1. *le point*
2. *la virgule*
3. *deux points*
4. *les guillemets*
5. *le point d'interrogation*
6. *points de suspension*
7. *point virgule*

____ semicolon
____ question mark
____ period
____ ellipses
____ quotation marks
____ comma
____ colon

§3.
ARTICLES

I. Write the appropriate definite article in front of each noun.

1. __ *garçon*   2. __ *jeune fille*   3. __ *arbre*
4. __ *livres*

II. Write the appropriate indefinite article in front of each noun.

5. __ *frère*   6. __ *sœur*   7. __ *frères*
8. __ *sœurs*

III. Write the French for the following phrases.

9. to Canada _____
10. to the United States _____
11. to the library _____
12. to the airport _____
13. from the United States _____
14. from Canada _____
15. the boy's book _____
16. the boys' books _____

IV. Write the French for the following sentences.

17. I have some coffee. _____
18. I don't have any coffee. _____
19. I have some meat. _____
20. I don't have any candies. _____

§4.
NOUNS

I. Write the definite article in front of each noun.

1. _____ homme   6. _____ chapeau
2. _____ femme   7. _____ chat
3. _____ coq   8. _____ gâteau
4. _____ vache   9. _____ âge
5. _____ poule   10. _____ sucette

II. Write the following nouns in the plural with the definite article.

11. le livre _____
12. l'étudiant _____
13. le journal _____
14. le bras _____
15. le bureau _____
16. l'œil _____
17. la voix _____
18. la maison _____
19. le ciel _____
20. le feu _____

§5.
ADJECTIVES

I. Supply the missing letters.

         EXAMPLE: les cie _ _   **Answer:** les cieux

1. Ce cra_on est mauv _ _ _.
2. Janine est aussi grand _ que Monique.
3. Jacqueline est plu _ joli _ que Simone.
4. Anne est absent _.

II. Complete each sentence with *ce, cet, cette,* or *ces.*

5. _____ garçon est beau.   6. _____ arbre est beau.
7. _____ livres sont beaux.   8. _____ femme est belle.

III. Complete each sentence with *belle, bel, beau,* or *beaux.*

9. Janine est une _____ jeune fille.
10. C'est un _____ arbre.
11. Jacques est un _____ jeune homme.
12. Ces livres sont _____.

IV. Supply the missing letters.

13. Joseph est acti _ et Joséphine est acti _ _.
14. Joseph et Joséphine jouent dans le jardin publi _ et dans cette long _ _ rue.
15. Joseph est heur _ _ _. Joséphine est heure _ _ _.
16. Il est genti _ et elle est gent _ _ _ _ _.

V. Complete the sentence with *vieux, vieil, vieille,* or *veille.*

La _____ dame a passé la _____ de Noël avec
　　　17.　　　　　　　　　　　18.

son _____ ami dans un _____ cabaret.
　　　19.　　　　　　　　　20.

§6.
PRONOUNS

I. *Mots-croisés* (Crossword Puzzle)

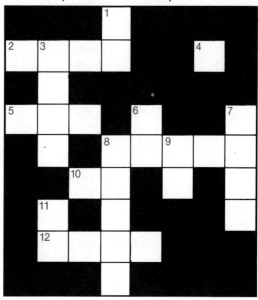

Verticalement

1. 1st person singular direct and indirect object pronoun.
3. 3d person plural indirect object pronoun.
6. Preposition used with adverbs of quantity, e.g., *beaucoup, trop.*
7. Masculine plural demonstrative pronoun.
8. Masculine singular demonstrative pronoun.
9. 3d person masculine singular direct object pronoun.
11. Pronoun that takes the place of the partitive and serves as a direct object.

Horizontalement

2. Feminine singular subject pronoun.
4. Pronoun commonly used in an interrogative sentence, as in *Est-ce qu'il...a?*
5. 3d person singular indirect object pronoun.
8. Feminine singular demonstrative pronoun.
10. 1st person singular subject pronoun.
12. 1st person plural direct and indirect object pronoun.

II. *La Roue de Fortune* (The Wheel of Fortune)
Complete each of the following by writing in the missing letters. Some letters are given to get you started. They are all pronouns.

1. *A __ C __ __ __*   4. *__ __ Q __ __ L L __*

2. *Q __ __ C __ __ Q __ __*   5. *__ A M __ __ N __ __*

3. *__ __ Q __ __ L*

§7.
VERBS

I. *Mots-croisés* (Crossword Puzzle)

Write the past participle for each of the following verbs.

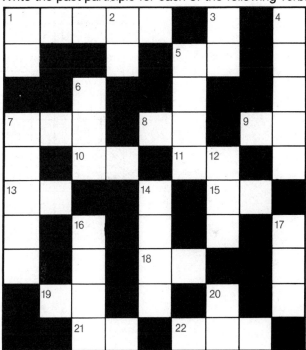

Verticalement

1. devoir	5. prendre	14. finir
2. naître	6. dire	16. mourir
3. lire	7. falloir	17. être
4. vendre	12. user	20. avoir

Horizontalement

1. donner	10. taire	18. naître
5. pouvoir	11. savoir	19. rire (à l'envers)*
7. fuir	13. lire	21. taire
8. rire	15. savoir	22. tuer
9. devoir (à l'envers)*		

* à l'envers / backwards

II. *Dans le potage* / In the soup. In this word puzzle, find
the present participle of each of the verbs listed below
and draw a line around each one. The first verb on the
list *(aller)*, whose present participle is *allant,* is already
done, to get you started. The words are written horizontally, vertically, or backwards.

C	H	A	N	T	A	N	T	A	T
H	F	Y	T	N	V	E	A	P	N
O	A	A	N	A	E	F	V	R	A
I	I	N	A	N	A	I	E	E	Y
S	S	T	Y	E	N	N	N	N	O
I	A	A	O	T	T	I	D	A	V
S	N	N	R	D	I	S	A	N	T
S	T	T	C	T	É	S	N	T	N
A	L	L	A	N	T	A	T	O	A
N	A	I	S	S	A	N	T	S	N
T	N	O	S	A	N	T	F	A	E
L	I	S	A	N	T	T	A	N	V

aller
avoir
chanter
choisir
croire
dire
être
faire
finir
lire
naître
oser
prendre
tenir
vendre
venir
voir

III. *Dans le potage.* In this word puzzle, find the verb form
in the present indicative tense for each verb in the
sentences below. When you find them, draw a line
around each one. The verb form in the present tense of
faire in the first statement given below is *faites*, and it
has already been done to get you started. The words
are written horizontally, vertically, diagonally, or backwards.

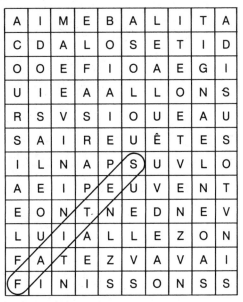

A	I	M	E	B	A	L	I	T	A
C	D	A	L	O	S	E	T	I	D
O	O	E	F	I	O	A	E	G	I
U	I	E	A	A	L	L	O	N	S
R	S	V	S	I	O	U	E	A	U
S	A	I	R	E	U	Ê	T	E	S
I	L	N	A	P	S	U	V	L	O
A	E	I	P	E	U	V	E	N	T
E	O	N	T	N	E	D	N	E	V
L	U	I	A	L	L	E	Z	O	N
F	A	T	E	Z	V	A	V	A	I
F	I	N	I	S	S	O	N	S	S

Que (faire)-vous ce soir?
Que me (dire)-vous?
J' (aimer) danser.
Moi, je (aller) chez moi.
Les garçons (avoir)-ils
    assez d'argent pour
    aller au cinéma?
Nous (aller) en France
    l'été prochain.
Quand (partir)-tu?
Et vous, (être)-vous
    heureux?
Tes parents (pouvoir)-ils
    venir avec nous?
Que (devoir)-tu faire
    maintenant?
Pourquoi (courir)-tu?
(Vendre)-ils leur maison?
Est-ce que nous (finir) le ⬅
    travail aujourd'hui?

IV. *Dans le potage.* Find the verb form in the imperfect indicative tense for each verb in the sentences below. When you find them, draw a line around each one. The verb form in the imperfect tense of *avoir* in the first statement given below is *avais,* and it is already done for you to get you started. The words are written horizontally and vertically.

A	V	A	I	S	É	T	I	E	Z
A	V	I	E	Z	É	T	A	I	T
F	A	I	S	I	E	Z	E	A	V
M	A	N	G	I	O	N	S	L	D
A	É	M	A	L	L	A	I	S	I
F	T	A	O	L	I	S	A	I	S
A	I	R	B	U	V	A	I	S	I
I	O	C	D	I	S	A	I	T	E
S	N	H	A	V	A	I	T	T	Z
A	S	A	L	L	I	O	N	S	S
I	A	I	P	A	R	L	A	I	S
S	I	T	R	O	U	V	A	I	T

Autrefois, lorsque j'
(avoir) dix ans, j'étais
très heureux.

Quand ma mère (être)
jeune, elle était belle.

Que (faire)-vous quand je
vous ai téléphoné?

Mon frère jouait pendant
que je (lire).

Nous (aller) à la plage
quand il a commencé à
pleuvoir.

Autrefois, je (boire) du vin
mais maintenant je
bois de l'eau.

Où (aller)-tu ce matin
quand je t'ai vu?

Dites-moi, lorsque Marie
(avoir) dix ans, allait-
elle souvent à la plage
avec ses copines?

Que (faire)-tu quand je
t'ai appelé?

L'homme (marcher)
lentement.

Que (dire)-vous quand
Robert vous a interrompu?

Nous (être) heureux
quand nous étions enfants.

La maison se (trouver) au
pied d'une montagne.

Nous (manger) quand tu
es arrivé.

Je (parler) souvent à
Jean mais je ne lui
parle plus maintenant.

Où (être)-vous à 20 h.
précises le soir du 15
novembre?

Que (dire) l'élève de
moi quand je suis entré
dans la salle de classe?

V. *Mots-croisés.* This activity tests your knowledge of the past indefinite tense. The missing words are the present tense of *avoir* or *être* or the correct form of the past participle, or a subject pronoun.

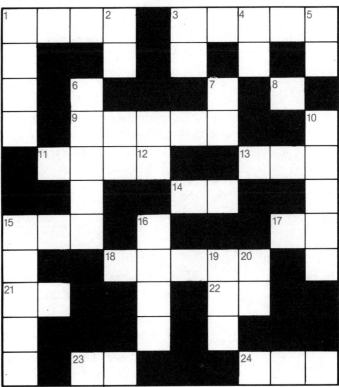

Horizontalement

1. *Hier, je _____ allé au cinéma.*
3. *Martine est _____ (aller) aux grands magasins.*
8. *Pierre _____ lu un livre.*
9. *Ils ont _____ (vouloir) partir.*
11. *_____ avez parlé assez.*
13. *La lettre? Je l'ai _____ (lire).*
14. *Pierre s'est _____ (taire).*
15. *J'ai _____ (mettre) du sucre dans le café.*
17. *J'ai _____ (devoir) (à l'envers)* partir.*
18. *Les lettres? Je les ai _____ (mettre) sur le bureau.*
21. *Nous avons bien _____ (rire).*
22. *Avez-vous _____ (savoir) la réponse?*
23. *Paul a-t- _____ compris?*
24. *Qu'a-t-elle _____ (dire)?*

* *à l'envers* / **backwards**

Verticalement

1. Je _____ tombé en montant dans le bus.
2. J'ai _____ (savoir) la réponse.
3. Hier soir, j'_____ beaucoup mangé.
4. Ma camarade a _____ (lire) un livre intéressant.
5. Ce matin j'ai _____ (avoir) un petit accident.
6. Nous _____ pris le train.
7. Les enfants ont _____ (pouvoir) manger.
10. Nous avons _____ (vendre) la maison.
12. A-t-il _____ (savoir) (à l'envers)* répondre à la question?
15. Madame Durand est _____ (mourir) la semaine dernière.
16. Tu as _____ (finir) la leçon?
19. Jacqueline _____ restée à la maison.
20. Tu as _____ (savoir) cela, n'est-ce pas?

*A l'envers/backwards

§8.
ADVERBS

I. Change the following adjectives into adverbs using the *-ment* ending in French.

1. gentil _____
2. franc _____
3. affreux _____
4. amer _____

II. Write at least ten common adverbs in French that do not end in *-ment.*

1. ____ 3. ____ 5. ____ 7. ____ 9. ____
2. ____ 4. ____ 6. ____ 8. ____ 10. ____

III. Unscramble the following letters to find an adverb in French. Then write it on the line provided.

| A H U E S M N M L E R U E E T | _____

IV. In this dialogue, Janine and you are talking about the exams in June and your summer vacation. Complete the conversation by choosing the appropriate French adverb from those given here.

bien   rapidement   récemment   toujours
aussi

Janine: Es-tu prêt pour tes examens?
Vous: Oui, je suis _____ prêt pour mes examens.
Janine: Demain j'ai encore un autre examen, et puis les vacances commencent.

> *Vous:*   *Les jours de vacances vont passer* _____.
> *Janine:*   *Nous avons passé l'été passé dans les*
>   *montagnes.*
> *Vous:*   *Ma famille et moi allons* _____ *dans les*
>   *montagnes.*
> *Janine:*   *En juillet nous allons faire un voyage en*
>   *Australie.*
> *Vous:*   *Ma famille et moi* _____ *! Nous allons à Mel-*
>   *bourne!*
> *Janine:*   *Si tu me donnes ton adresse, je vais t'envoyer*
>   *une carte postale de Sydney.*
> *Vous:*   *Mais je t'ai donné* _____ *mon adresse! L'as-tu*
>   *perdue?*

§9. PREPOSI-TIONS

Hidden words. Among the following prepositions numbered 1 to 6, some are hidden in the block of words given below, but some are not. Which of these prepositions are not in the block of words?

1. *dans*   2. *en*   3. *vers*
4. *envers*   5. *pour*   6. *pendant*

> POURQUOI LA PORTE UNE HEURE AIMER AVEC
> SOIR CHAQUE PAR ENVERS SANS DE DENT OU
> PARCE QUE VERS AN PENDANT PROBABLEMENT

Solution: The prepositions that are not in the block of words are the ones numbered: _____

§10. CONJUNC-TIONS

I. In the following paragraph, underline all the conjunctions that you find and write them on the lines below.

> *Je ne peux pas aller à la surprise-partie chez Jim ce*
> *soir parce que j'ai beaucoup de devoirs à faire et,*
> *comme mon père est malade, je dois rester à la maison;*
> *mais demain c'est possible ou dans trois jours.*

_____   _____

_____   _____

II. Complete the following French conjunctions.

1. *à moins* _____ / unless
2. *de* _____ *que* / for fear that
3. *en même* _____ *que* / at the same time as
4. *jusqu'à* _____ *que* / until
5. _____ *que* / whereas

III. A Letter Clock. Three conjunctions in French are hidden in this clock; one conjunction from 12 to 6; one from 4 to 6; and another from 6 to 11. Note that the same letter can be common to the one that follows. This clock has no hands because it's a "word clock." Write the missing letters on the lines.

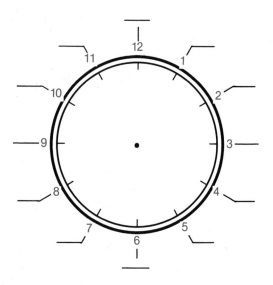

CLUES:

From 12 to 6, give the French for the conjunction "when" that is a synonym of *quand*.

From 4 to 6, give the French for the conjunction "that."

From 6 to 11, give the French for the conjunction "at the same time as."

(There was no more room in the clock to write *temps que* to complete that conjunction!)

§11.
ORDER OF ELEMENTS IN FRENCH SENTENCES

I. Unscramble the words to form a coherent sentence.

1. *me / ne / donne / les / Elle / pas* _____
2. *pas / ne / leur / le / Je / donne* _____
3. *leur / Ne / les / pas / donnez* _____
4. *s' / pas / est / lavée / ne / Elle* _____
5. *pas / ai / lui / donné / Je / le / ne* _____

§12.
IDIOMS

Each of the following sentences contains a blank. Of the three choices given, select the one that can be inserted in the blank to form a grammatically correct sentence and circle the letter of your choice.

1. _____ *quand habitez-vous cet appartement?*
   A. *Pour*   B. *Depuis*   C. *Combien de temps*

2. *J'habite cet appartement* _____ *le vingt-deux août, 1966.*
   A. *depuis*   B. *pour*   C. *il y a*

3. _____ *quand êtes-vous malade?*
   A. *Depuis*   B. *Combien de temps*   C. *Pour*

4. *Je suis malade* _____ *samedi.*
   A. *combien*   B. *depuis*   C. *de*

5. *J'habitais l'appartement* _____ *le cinq avril 1987 quand j'ai déménagé.*
   A. *pour*   B. *depuis combien de temps*   C. *depuis*

II. Write the missing word or words in order to complete each of the following basic idiomatic expressions. Choose from among the following:

à   au   aux   aller   avoir   d'   de   du   être   faire

1. _____ *vélo*
2. _____ *téléphone*
3. _____ *pommes frites*
4. _____ *pied*
5. _____ *faim*
6. *comme* _____ *habitude*
7. *changer* _____ *train*
8. _____ *en retard*
9. _____ *un voyage*
10. _____ *une promenade*
11. _____ *lieu de*
12. _____ *partir de*
13. _____ *chercher*
14. _____ *besoin de*
15. _____ *soif*
16. _____ *bonne heure*
17. *tout* _____ *un coup*
18. _____ *en train de*
19. _____ *les valises*
20. *Que* _____ *?*

§13.
DATES, DAYS, MONTHS, SEASONS

I. Each of the following sentences contains a blank. Of the four choices given, select the one that can be inserted in the blank to form a sensible and grammatically correct sentence and circle the letter of your choice.

1. *Quelle est la date aujourd'hui? C'est aujourd'hui* _____ *février.*
   A. *l'un*   B. *le premier de*   C. *le premier*
   D. *la première*

2. *Quel jour précède lundi? C'est* _____.
   A. *samedi*　　**B.** *dimanche*　　**C.** *mardi*
   D. *jeudi*

3. *Il y a* _____ *saisons dans l'année.*
   A. *cinq*　　**B.** *quart*　　**C.** *quatre*　　**D.** *quarante*

4. *Les fleurs poussent* _____ *printemps.*
   A. *en*　　**B.** *dans*　　**C.** *dans le*　　**D.** *au*

5. *En général,* _____ *hiver il fait froid à New York.*
   A. *en*　　**B.** *dans*　　**C.** *dans l'*　　**D.** *à l'*

§14.
TELLING TIME

I. Study the clocks and below each one write the time that is given in French words.

A. 　　B. 　　C.

_____　　_____　　_____

D. 　　E. 　　F.

_____　　_____　　_____

§15.
TALKING ABOUT THE WEATHER

I. Read the statement in English and then select the correct equivalent in French by drawing a circle around the letter of your choice.

1. What's the weather like today?
   A. *Fait-il beau temps aujourd'hui?*
   B. *Quel temps fait-il aujourd'hui?*
   C. *Fait-il un temps affreux aujourd'hui?*
   D. *Quelle heure est-il?*

2. It's very warm today.
   A. *Il fait très beau aujourd'hui.*
   B. *Il fait chaud aujourd'hui.*
   C. *Il fait très chaud aujourd'hui.*
   D. *Il fait très froid aujourd'hui.*

3. It's muggy.
   A. *Il fait un temps couvert.*
   B. *Le temps menace.*
   C. *Le temps se met au beau.*
   D. *Il fait un temps lourd.*

4. It's windy.
   A. *Il fait du tonnerre.*
   B. *Il fait du vent.*
   C. *Il grêle.*
   D. *Il pleut.*

5. It's raining.
   A. *Il neige.*
   B. *Il fait mauvais.*
   C. *Il gèle.*
   D. *Il pleut.*

II. Weather Announcement. Place the four numbered blocks vertically in the right spot next to the second column of letters, and you will read the weather announcement. The announcement reads vertically.

1. | O L | | I |
2. | L F | | A I |
3. | L | | U S |
4. | T D | | E I |

§16.
NUMBERS

I. Each of the following sentences contains a blank. Of the four choices given, select the one that can be inserted in the blank to form a sensible and grammatically correct sentence and circle the letter of your choice.

1. *Douze et treize font* _____ .
   A. *vingt-deux*   B. *quinze*
   C. *cinquante-deux*   D. *vingt-cinq*

2. *Dix* _____ *quatre font six.*
   A. *et*   **B.** *fois*   **C.** *moins*   **D.** *divisés par*

3. *Cinq* _____ *seize font quatre-vingts.*
   A. *et*   **B.** *fois*   **C.** *moins*   **D.** *divisés par*

4. *Seize* _____ *huit font deux.*
   A. *et*   **B.** *fois*   **C.** *moins*   **D.** *divisés par*

5. *Cinq cents* _____ *deux font deux cent cinquante.*
   A. *et*   **B.** *fois*   **C.** *moins*   **D.** *divisés par*

II. Match the following.

1. *un quart*   _____ *one-fourth*
2. *un demi*   _____ *one-fifth*
3. *un cinquième*   _____ *one-half*
4. *un tiers*   _____ *one-third*

§17. SYNONYMS

I. Match the following synonyms.

1. *aide*   _____ *docteur*
2. *anneau*   _____ *avis*
3. *souci*   _____ *détester*
4. *médecin*   _____ *chaussure*
5. *haïr*   _____ *favori*
6. *préféré*   _____ *car*
7. *conseil*   _____ *secours*
8. *parce que*   _____ *chagrin*
9. *soulier*   _____ *donner un baiser*
10. *embrasser*   _____ *bague*

II. Write the missing letters on the lines.

1. __ R __ V __ __ L __ E R
2. D __ S __ R __ R
3. P __ __ F __ S __ E __ R
4. B __ T __ __ E __ T
5. M I __ I __ U
6. H __ B __ T E __

§18. ANTONYMS

I. Several words in one. Using the letters in the word *PARESSEUSE*, how many words can you find within it? Write at least six.

PARESSEUSE

1. _____   3. _____   5. _____
2. _____   4. _____   6. _____

II. Several words in one. Using the letters in the word *MAISON,* how many words can you find within it? Write at least six.

1. _____ 3. _____ 5. _____
2. _____ 4. _____ 6. _____

Now rearrange all the letters in the word *MAISON* and find another French word that contains the same letters. The new word is: _____

III. Match the following. They are all antonyms.

1. *étroit*   _____ *derrière*
2. *grand*   _____ *dehors*
3. *gai*   _____ *fausse*
4. *dedans*   _____ *petit*
5. *beauté*   _____ *naître*
6. *vraie*   _____ *laideur*
7. *ami*   _____ *sur*
8. *devant*   _____ *large*
9. *sous*   _____ *ennemi*
10. *mourir*   _____ *triste*

§19.
COGNATES

I. Write the English word for the following French words.

1. *honnête* _____   6. *bâtiment* _____
2. *pâte* _____   7. *gâteau* _____
3. *bête* _____   8. *âme* _____
4. *forêt* _____   9. *aimable* _____
5. *prêtre* _____   10. *permettre* _____

II. Alphabet Soup. Find the French words for the English cognates given below and circle each one. They are horizontal, vertical, and backwards.

A	E	L	B	A	M	I	A	P
P	A	T	P	L	Â	T	R	E
A	D	M	E	T	T	R	E	A
E	T	Â	P	E	T	Â	H	A

admit   mast   amiable   plaster   paste   haste

§20. TRICKY WORDS

I. Write the French word and its definite article for each of the following.

EXAMPLE: pen   You write: *le stylo*

1. sound _____
2. news reports _____
3. plum _____
4. thing _____
5. goal _____

6. prune _____
7. bread _____
8. store _____
9. arrow _____
10. bear (animal) _____

II. Match the following tricky French words with their English equivalents.

1. *le chat*
2. *causer*
3. *le front*
4. *large*
5. *la chair*
6. *blesser*
7. *bénir*
8. *le cabinet*
9. *sale*
10. *le sable*

_____ dirty
_____ flesh
_____ sand
_____ wide
_____ to wound
_____ forehead
_____ office or study
_____ cat
_____ to bless
_____ to chat

Answers

§1.
**PRONOUNC-
ING FRENCH
SOUNDS**

1. A.   2. A.   3. A.   4. A.   5. A.   6. A.
7. A.   8. A.   9. C.   10. D.
Review §1.

§2.
**CAPITALIZA-
TION, PUNC-
TUATION
MARKS,
WORD
DIVISION**

I. 1. *é / cole*   2. *im / por / tant*   3. *a / près*
II. 7, 5, 1, 6, 4, 2, 3   Review §2.

§3.
ARTICLES

I.   1. *le*   2. *la*   3. *l'*   4. *les*   Review §3.1.

II. 5. *un*   6. *une*   7. *des*   8. *des*   Review §3.2.

III. 9. *au Canada*
     10. *aux Etats-Unis*
     11. *à la bibliothèque*
     12. *à l'aéroport*
     13. *des Etats-Unis*
     14. *du Canada*
     15. *le livre du garçon*
     16. *les livres des garçons*
     Review §3.1.

IV. 17. *J'ai du café.*
     18. *Je n'ai pas de café.*
     19. *J'ai de la viande.*
     20. *Je n'ai pas de bonbons.*
     Review §3.3.

§4.
NOUNS

I. 1. *l'*   2. *la*   3. *le*   4. *la*   5. *la*   6. *le*
   7. *le*   8. *le*   9. *l'*   10. *la*   Review §4.1.

II. 11. *les livres*   17. *les voix*
    12. *les étudiants*   18. *les maisons*
    13. *les journaux*   19. *les cieux*
    14. *les bras*   20. *les feux*
    15. *les bureaux*   Review §4.2.
    16. *les yeux*

§5.
ADJECTIVES

I. 1. *y; a, i, s*   2. *e*   3. *s; e*   4. *e*
   Review §5.1 & §5.2.

II. 5. *ce*   6. *cet*   7. *ces*   8. *cette*
    Review §5.4 – 2.

III. 9. *belle*   10. *bel*   11. *beau*   12. *beaux*
     Review §5.1.

IV. 13. *f; v, e*   14. *c; u, e*   15. *e, u, x; u, s, e*
    16. *l; i, l, l, e*   Review §5.1.

V. 17. *vieille*   18. *veille*   19. *vieil*   20. *vieux*
   Review §5.1.

§6.
PRONOUNS

I. Review §6. – §6.1 – 8 for this crossword puzzle.

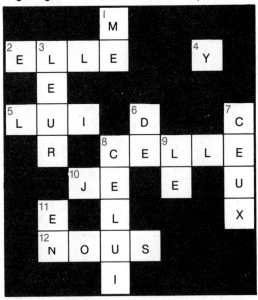

II. 1. U, U, N *(aucun)* Review §6.1 – 9.
    2. U, I, O, N, U, E *(quiconque)* Review §6.1 – 9.
    3. L, E, U, E *(lequel)* Review §6.1 – 10.
    4. L, A, U, E, E *(laquelle)* Review §6.1 – 10.
    5. L,   I, E, N, E *(la mienne)* Review §6.1 – 11.

§7.
VERBS

I. Review §7.2 for this crossword puzzle.

1 D	O	N	2 N	É		3 L		4 V
Û			É		5 P	U		E
		6 D			R			N
7 F	U	I		8 R	I		9 Û	D
A		10 T	U		11 S	12 U		U
13 L	U			14 F		15 S	U	
L		16 M		I		É		17 É
U		O		18 N	É			T
	19 I	R		I		20 E		É
	21 T	U		22 T	U	É		

II. Review §7.4 for the present participles in this word puzzle.

C	H	A	N	T	A	N	T	A	T
H	F	Y	T	N	V	E	A	P	M
O	A	A	N	A	E	F	V	R	A
I	I	N	A	N	A	I	E	E	Y
S	S	T	Y	E	N	N	N	N	O
I	A	A	O	T	T	I	D	A	V
S	N	N	R	D	I	S	A	N	T
S	T	T	C	T	É	S	N	T	N
A	L	L	A	N	T	A	T	O	A
N	A	I	S	S	A	N	T	S	N
T	N	O	S	A	N	T	F	A	E
L	I	S	A	N	T	T	A	N	V

III. Review §7.8–1 & §7.17 for the present indicative tense of verbs in this word puzzle.

A	I	M	E	B	A	L	I	T	A
C	D	A	L	O	S	E	T	I	D
O	O	E	F	I	O	A	E	G	I
U	I	E	A	A	L	L	O	N	S
R	S	V	S	I	O	U	E	A	U
S	A	I	R	E	U	Ê	T	E	S
I	L	N	A	P	S	U	V	L	O
A	E	I	P	E	U	V	E	N	T
E	O	N	T	N	E	D	N	E	V
L	U	I	A	L	L	E	Z	O	N
F	A	T	E	Z	V	A	V	A	I
F	I	N	I	S	S	O	N	S	S

IV. Review §7.8–2 & §7.17 for the imperfect indicative tense of verbs in this word puzzle.

A	V	A	I	S	É	T	I	E	Z
A	V	I	E	Z	É	T	A	I	T
F	A	I	S	I	E	Z	E	A	V
M	A	N	G	I	O	N	S	L	D
A	É	M	A	L	L	A	I	S	I
F	T	A	O	L	I	S	A	I	S
A	I	R	B	U	V	A	I	S	I
I	O	C	D	I	S	A	I	T	E
S	N	H	A	V	A	I	T	T	Z
A	S	A	L	L	I	O	N	S	S
I	A	I	P	A	R	L	A	I	S
S	I	T	R	O	U	V	A	I	T

V. Review §7.1, §7.2, §7.3–1, §7.8–8, §7.17 for the past indefinite *(passé composé)* of verbs in this crossword puzzle.

¹S	U	I	²S	■	³A	L	L	⁴É	⁵E
U	■	■	U	■	I	■	■	U	U
I	■	⁶A	■	■	■	⁷P	■	⁸A	■
S	■	⁹V	O	U	L	U	■	■	¹⁰V
■	¹¹V	O	U	¹²S	■	■	¹³L	U	E
■	■	N	■	■	¹⁴T	U	■	■	N
¹⁵M	I	S	■	¹⁶F	■	■	¹⁷Û	■	D
O	■	■	¹⁸M	I	S	¹⁹E	²⁰S	■	U
²¹R	I	■	■	N	■	²²S	U	■	■
T	■	■	■	I	■	T	■	■	■
E	■	²³I	L	■	■	²⁴D	I	T	

§8.
ADVERBS

I. 1. *gentiment*   2. *franchement*   3. *affreusement*
    4. *amèrement*   Review §8.1.

II. 1. *bien*   2. *mal*   3. *vite*   4. *combien*
     5. *comment*   6. *pourquoi*   7. *où*
     8. *quand*   9. *beaucoup*   10. *assez*
     Review §8.1, §8.3–1.

III. *malheureusement*   Review §8.1, §8.2.

IV. *bien; rapidement; toujours; aussi; récemment*
     Review §8.–§8.3.

§9.
PREPOSI-
TIONS—
SPECIAL USES

1, 2, 5. Review §9.

§10. CONJUNC- TIONS

I. *parce que; et; comme; mais; ou*   **Review §10.**

II. **1.** *que*   **2.** *peur (crainte)*   **3.** *temps*   **4.** *ce*
    5. *tandis*   **Review §10.**

III.

§11. ORDER OF ELEMENTS IN FRENCH SENTENCES

I. **1.** *Elle ne me les donne pas.*   **4.** *Elle ne s'est pas lavée.*
  2. *Je ne le leur donne pas.*   **5.** *Je ne le lui ai pas donné.*
  3. *Ne les leur donnez pas.*   **Review §11.**

§12. IDIOMS

I. **1.** B   **2.** A   **3.** A   **4.** B   **5.** C
  Review §12.1.

II. **1.** *à*   **2.** *au*   **3.** *aux*   **4.** *à*   **5.** *avoir*
  6. *d'*   **7.** *de*   **8.** *être*   **9.** *faire*   **10.** *faire*
  11. *au*   **12** *à*   **13.** *aller*   **14.** *avoir*
  15. *avoir*   **16.** *de*   **17.** *d'*   **18.** *être*
  19. *faire*   **20.** *faire*   **Review §12.2.**

§13. DATES, DAYS, MONTHS, SEASONS

I. **1.** C   **2.** B   **3.** C   **4.** D   **5.** A
  Review §13.

§14. TELLING TIME

A.

Il est cinq heures dix.

B.

Il est une heure.

C.

Il est six heures moins le quart.

D.

Il est sept heures et demie.

E.

Il est onze heures et quart.

F.

Il est quatre heures et quart.

Review §14.

§15. TALKING ABOUT THE WEATHER

I. 1. B   2. C   3. D   4. B   5. D

II. *Il fait du soleil.*

I | L F

A I | T D

U S | O L

E I | L

Review §15.

§16. NUMBERS

I. 1. D   2. C   3. B   4. D   5. D

II. 1, 3, 2, 4

Review §16.

§17. SYNONYMS

I. 4, 7, 5, 9, 6, 8, 1, 3, 10, 2

II. 1. T, A, A, I, L *(travailler)*
2. É, I, E *(désirer)*
3. R, O, E, S, U *(profes-seur)*
4. Â, I, M, N *(bâtiment)*
5. L, E *(milieu)*
6. A, I, R *(habiter)*

Review §17.

§18.
ANTONYMS

I. 1. *par*   2. *eu*   3. *se*   4. *rue*   5. *su*
6. *paresse*

II. 1. *ma*   2. *si*   3. *son*   4. *mais*   5. *nom*
6. *ai*

The new word is: *AIMONS* Let's love.)

III. 8, 4, 6, 2, 10, 5, 9, 1, 7, 3

§19.
COGNATES

I. 1. honest   2. paste   3. beast   4. forest
5. priest   6. building   7. cake   8. soul
9. amiable (likeable)   10. to permit

II.

A	E	L	B	A	M	I	A	P
P	A	T	P	L	Â	T	R	E
A	D	M	E	T	T	R	E	A
E	T	Â	P	E	T	Â	H	A

Review §19.

§20.
TRICKY
WORDS

I. 1. *le son*   2. *les actualités*   3. *la prune*
4. *la chose*   5. *le but*   6. *le pruneau*   7. *le pain*   8. *le magasin*   9. *la flèche*   10. *l'ours*

II. 9, 5, 10, 4, 6, 3, 8, 1, 7, 2
Review §20.

French-English Vocabulary

à *prep.* at, to
à moins que *conj.* unless
actif, active *adj.* active
aéroport *n.m.* airport
affreusement *adv.* frightfully
ai *v. form of* **avoir**
aimable *adj.* amiable, likeable, pleasant, kind
aimer *v.* to love; **aimer bien** to like
Allemagne *n.f.* Germany
allemand *n.m.* German (language); **Allemand, Allemande** *n.* German (person)
aller *v.* to go; **s'en aller** to go away
allez-vous-en! go away!
allons! let's go!
amèrement *adv.* bitterly
ami, amie *n.* friend
amour *n.m.* love
amusant, amusante *adj.* funny, amusing
an *n.m.* year
ancien, ancienne *adj.* old, ancient
anglais *n.m.* English (language); **Anglais, Anglaise** *n.* English (person)
Angleterre *n.f.* England
appeler *v.* to call; **s'appeler** *reflexive v.* to call oneself, to be named
après *prep., adv.* after; **après-midi** afternoon
arbre *n.m.* tree
argent *n.m.* money
Asie *n.f.* Asia
asseoir *v.* to seat; **s'asseoir** *reflexive v.* to sit down; **asseyez-vous!** sit down!
assez (de) *adv.* enough (of); **assez bien** quite well, well enough
assieds-toi! sit down!
au to the, at the; contraction of **à + le**
aujourd'hui *adv.* today
aussi *adv.* also, too
aussi . . . que *conj.* as . . . as
Australie *n.f.* Australia
auteur *n.m.* author; **une femme auteur** woman author
autre *adj.* other; *pron.* another
autrefois *adv.* formerly

aux to the, at the; contraction of **à + les**
avec *prep.* with
avez *v. form of* **avoir**
avocat *n.m.* lawyer; **une avocate** woman lawyer
avoir *v.* to have

bas *n.m.* stocking; *adv.* low; **en bas** down, downstairs; *adj.* **bas, basse** low
beau *adj. m.* handsome, beautiful
beaucoup (de) *adv.* many, much (of)
bel *adj. m.* handsome, beautiful
belle *adj. f.* beautiful, handsome
bénir *v.* to bless
besoin *n.m.* need; **avoir besoin de** to need, to have need of
bibliothèque *n.f.* library
bien *adv.* well
bientôt *adv.* soon
billet *n.m.* ticket, note
blanc, blanche *adj.* white
blesser *v.* to injure, to wound
boire *v.* to drink
bon, bonne *adj.* good
bonbons *n.m.* candies
bouche *n.f.* mouth (of a person); **la gueule** (mouth of an animal)
but *n.m* goal

ça *pron.* shortening of **cela**
cadeau *n.m.* gift, present
café *n.m.* coffee
cahier *n.m.* notebook
campagne *n.f.* country(side)
catholique *n.m.f.* Catholic
ce *demons. adj.* this; **ce stylo** this pen; **ce livre** this book; **ce garçon** this boy
cela *pron.* that; **Aimez-vous cela?** Do you like that?
chanter *v.* to sing
chanteur, chanteuse *n.m.f.* singer

---

adj.: adjective; adv.: adverb; conj.: conjunction; f.: feminine; m.: masculine; n.: noun; pl.: plural; prep.: preposition; pron.: pronoun; sing.: singular; v.: verb

chapeau *n.m.* hat
chaque *adj.* each
chaud, chaude *adj.* warm, hot
chaussette *n.f.* sock
chaussure *n.f.* shoe
chef *n.m.* chief, boss, chef
cheveu, cheveux *n.m.* hair
chez *prep.* at the place of, at the home of, at the shop of; **chez moi** at my place
choisir *v.* to choose, to select
chose *n.f.* thing; **quelque chose** something
cinéma *n.m.* movies (theater)
clé, clef *n.f.* key
coin *n.m.* corner
combien (de) *adv.* how much (of), how many (of)
comprendre *v.* to understand
copain *n.m.,* **copine** *n.f.* pal, buddy
cravate *n.f.* necktie
crayon *n.m.* pencil
croire *v.* to believe
cruel, cruelle *adj.* cruel

dame *n.f.* lady
dans *prep.* in
de *prep.* of, from
dehors *adv.* outside
déjà *adv.* already; **déjà vu** already seen
dent *n.f.* tooth
depuis *adv.* since; **depuis longtemps** for a long time
dernier, dernière *adj.* last
des of the, from the; contraction of **de + les;** some
dimanche *n.m.* Sunday
dire *v.* to say, to tell; **vouloir dire** to mean
donc *conj.* therefore, consequently
donner *v.* to give
dont *pron.* of which, whose
dormir *v.* to sleep
douche *n.f.* shower (bath)
douter *v.* to doubt
drôle *adj.* funny, droll
du of the, from the; contraction of **de + le;** some
dû *past participle of* **devoir;** ought to, must

eau *n.f.* water
école *n.f.* school; **à l'école** in (at, to) school
écouter *v.* to listen (to)
écrire *v.* to write
écrivons *v. form of* **écrire**

égal, égaux, égale, égales *adj.* equal
église *n.f.* church
en *pron.* of it, of them, some of it, some of them; *prep.* in
encore *adv.* still, yet, again
encre *n.f.* ink
enregistrer *v.* to record (on a tape, record)
enseigner *v.* to teach
entendre *v.* to hear, to understand
enthousiasme *n.m.* enthusiasm
entre *prep.* between; *also a v. form of* **entrer (dans)** to enter (into)
envers *prep.* toward
environ *adv.* nearly, about
envoyer *v.* to send; **envoyer chercher** to send for
Espagne *n.f.* Spain
espagnol *n.m.* Spanish (language); **Espagnol, Espagnole** *n.* Spanish (person)
est *present indicative of* **être**
Etats-Unis *n.m.pl.* United States
été *n.m.* summer; *also past participle of* **être**
être *v.* to be
étudiant, étudiante *n.m.* student
étudier *v.* to study
eu *past participle of* **avoir**

faim *n.f.* hunger; **avoir faim** to be hungry
faire *v.* to do, to make; **faire un voyage** to take a trip
falloir *v.* to be necessary; **il faut** it is necessary
faux, fausse *adj.* false
favori, favorite *adj.* favorite
femme *n.f.* woman; when possessive, wife **ma femme** my wife
fête *n.f.* feast, holiday, party
feu *n.m.* fire; **le feu rouge** red light (traffic)
février *n.m.* February
fille *n.f.* daughter; **la jeune fille** girl; **une école de filles** girls' school
fils *n.m.* son
finir *v.* to finish, to end
forêt *n.f.* forest
fourchette *n.f.* fork
français *n.m.* French (language); **Français, Française** *n.* French (person)
franchement *adv.* frankly
frère *n.m.* brother
fromage *n.m.* cheese
fuir *v.* to flee, to run away; *past participle* **fu**

garçon *n.m.* boy
gâteau *n.m.* cake
gentil, gentille *adj.* nice, pleasant
gentiment *adv.* gently
gomme *n.f.* eraser (rubber)
grand, grande *adj.* great, big, large; **un grand magasin** department store
Grande Bretagne *n.f.* Great Britain
gris, grise *adj.* gray
gros, grosse *adj.* big, fat, large

heureusement *adv.* fortunately, happily
heureux, heureuse *adj.* happy
homme *n.m.* man
honneur *n.m.* honor
huître *n.f.* oyster

ici *adv.* here
île *n.f.* isle, island
immeuble *n.m.* apartment building
interrompre *v.* to interrupt
italien *n.m.* Italian (language); **Italien, Italienne** *n.* Italian (person)

janvier *n.m.* January
jeune *adj.* young
jeune fille *n.f.* girl
joli, jolie *adj.* pretty
jouer *v.* to play
jouet *n.m.* toy
jour *n.m.* day
journal *n.m.* newspaper
journée *n.f.* (all) day (long)

la *definite article, f.* the; *also direct object pronoun, f. sing.* it, her
laid, laide *adj.* ugly
laideur *n.f.* ugliness
laver *v.* to wash (something or someone); **se laver** *reflex. verb* to wash oneself
le *definite article, m.* the; *also direct object pronoun, m. sing.* it, him
lent, lente *adj.* slow
lentement *adv.* slowly
les *definite article, m. and f.* the; *also direct object pronoun, m. and f., pl.* them (people or things)

leur *possessive adj.* their; *also indirect object pron.* to them
lire *v.* to read; *past participle* **lu**
lit *n.m.* bed; *also present indicative, 3d person sing.* of **lire**
livre *n.m.* book; **la livre** pound
Londres *n.m.* London
long, longue *adj.* long
longtemps *adv.* long time; **depuis longtemps** since a long time, for a long time
lorsque *adv.* when; *synonym of* **quand**
lui *indirect object pron., 3d person sing.* to him, to her
lundi *n.m.* Monday

ma *possessive adj., f. sing.* my; **ma maison** my house
magasin *n.m.* store; **un grand magasin** department store
magazine *n.m.* magazine
maintenant *adv.* now
mais *conj.* but
maison *n.f.* house
malheur *n.m.* unhappiness
malheureusement *n.f.* unfortunately
manger *v.* to eat
marcher *v.* to walk, to march, to run (a machine)
mardi *n.m.* Tuesday
mars *n.m.* March
matin *n.m.* morning; **le matin** in the morning
médecin *n.m.* doctor
médecine *n.f.* medicine (profession)
médicament *n.m.* medicine (that you take)
meilleur, meilleure *adj.* better
mer *n.f.* sea
mère *n.f.* mother
mettre *v.* to put, to place; to put on (clothing)
mieux *adv.* better
monnaie *n.f.* change (money); coins
monsieur *n.m.* gentleman, sir, Mr.
mourir *v.* to die

naître *v.* to be born; *past participle* **né**
natation *n.f.* swimming
noir, noire *adj.* black
nom *n.m.* name
nouveau, nouvel, nouvelle *adj.* new

œil *n.m.* eye; **les yeux** eyes
œuf *n.m.* egg
oiseau *n.m.* bird
on *personal pron., 3d person sing.* one (they)
oser *v.* to dare
ou *conj.* or; **où** *adv.* where
ouvrir *v.* to open; *past participle* **ouvert**

pain *n.m.* bread
papier *n.m.* paper
par *prep.* by; **par terre** on the floor, on the ground
parapluie *n.m.* umbrella
parc *n.m.* park
paresse *n.f.* laziness
paresseux, paresseuse *adj.* lazy
parler *v.* to talk, to speak
partir *v.* to leave; *past participle* **parti**
passer *v.* to spend (time); to go by, to pass by, to pass
pendant *prep.* during; **pendant que** *conj.* while
perdre *v.* to lose; *past participle* **perdu(e)(s)**
père *n.m.* father
perspicacité *n.f.* perspicacity, insight
peu (de) *adv.* little (of)
peur *n.f.* fear; **avoir peur** to be afraid, to feel afraid
peut *present indicative of* **pouvoir**
pied *n.m.* foot; **aller à pied** to walk
plage *n.f.* beach, seashore
pleuvoir *v.* to rain; *past participle* **plu**
plus *adv.* more; **plus de, plus que** more than
plusieurs *adv.* several
poule *n.f.* hen
poupée *n.f.* doll
pousser *v.* to push, to bud (flowers)
pouvoir *v.* to be able, can
précise *adj.* precise, precisely
prendre *v.* to take
presse *n.f.* press (printing)
public, publique *adj.* public
puis *adv.* then

quand *adv.* when; *synonym of* **lorsque**
quel, quelle, quels, quelles *adj.* which, what
quelque(s) *adj.* some; **quelque chose** something
quelquefois *adv.* sometimes
qui *pron.* who, whom

qui est-ce qui *pron.* who
quitter *v.* to leave (a person or place)
quoi *pron.* what (as obj. of a prep.); **avec quoi** with what

rang *n.m.* rank, row
restaurant *n.m.* restaurant
rire *v.* to laugh; laughter
robe *n.f.* dress
rose *n.f.* rose; *adj.* pink
rue *n.f.* street

samedi *n.m.* Saturday
sans *prep.* without
se *reflexive pron.* himself, herself, oneself
sec, sèche *adj.* dry
seize sixteen
semaine *n.f.* week
si *conj.* if
sœur *n.f.* sister
soir *n.m.* evening; **le soir** in the evening
son *n.m.* sound; *possessive adj.* his, her, its
sont *v. form of* **être**
sous *prep.* under
souvent *adv.* often
stylo *n.m.* pen
sucette *n.f.* lollipop; **sucer** *v.* to suck
sur *prep.* on

tenir *v.* to hold
thé *n.m.* tea
très *adv.* very
trop (de) *adv.* too much (of), too many (of)
trouver *v.* to find; **se trouver** *reflexive v.* to be located
tuer *v.* to kill

un *indefinite article, m. sing.* a, an (one); *fem.,* **une**

vacances *n.f.pl.* vacation; **les grandes vacances** summer vacation
vache *n.f.* cow
vais *present indicative of* **aller**

vendre *v.* to sell
venir *v.* to come
vent *n.m.* wind; **il fait du vent** it's windy
viande *n.f.* meat
vient *present indicative of* **venir**
vieux, vieil, vieille *adj.* old
vin *n.m.* wine
vingt twenty
voir *v.* to see; *past participle* **vu**

voyage *n.m.* trip; **faire un voyage** to take a trip, go on a trip; **Bon voyage!** Have a good trip!

y *adverbial pron.* there, in it, on it
yeux *n.m.* eyes; **l'œil** the eye

zèbre *n.m.* zebra

Index

References are to § numbers in this book. There are also some references to page numbers.

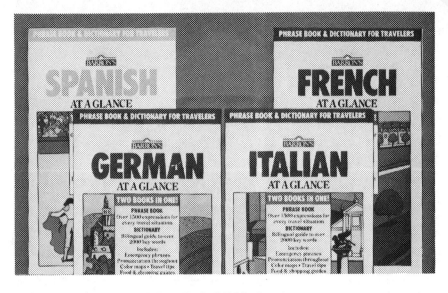

FOREIGN PHRASE BOOKS *Series*

Barron's new series gives travelers instant access to the most common idiomatic expressions used during a trip—the kind one needs to know instantly, like "Where can I find a taxi?" and "How much does this cost?"

Organized by situation (arrival, customs, hotel, health, etc.) and containing additional information about pronunciation, grammar, shopping plus special facts about the country, these convenient, pocket-size reference books will be the tourist's most helpful guides.

Special features include a bilingual dictionary section with over 2000 key words, maps of each country and major cities, and helpful phonetic spellings throughout.

Each book paperback, 256 pp., 3 3/4" x 6"

ARABIC AT A GLANCE, Wise (2979-8) $5.95, Can. $7.95
CHINESE AT A GLANCE, Seligman, Chen (2851-1) $6.95, Can. $9.95
FRENCH AT A GLANCE, 2nd, Stein & Wald (1394-8) $5.95, Can. $7.95
GERMAN AT A GLANCE, 2nd, Strutz (1395-6) $5.95, Can. $7.95
ITALIAN AT A GLANCE, 2nd, Costantino (1396-4) $5.95, Can. $7.95
JAPANESE AT A GLANCE, 2nd, Akiyama (1397-2) $6.95, Can. $8.95
KOREAN AT A GLANCE, Holt (3998-X) $8.95, Can. $10.95
RUSSIAN AT A GLANCE, Beyer (4299-9) $5.95, Can. $7.95
SPANISH AT A GLANCE, 2nd, Wald (1398-0) $5.95, Can. $7.95

BARRON'S

Barron's Educational Series, Inc.
250 Wireless Blvd., Hauppauge, NY 11788
Call toll-free: 1-800-645-3476
In Canada: Georgetown Book Warehouse, 34 Armstrong Ave.
Georgetown, Ont. L7G 4R9, Call toll-free: 1-800-247-7160

Books may be purchased at your bookstore, or by mail from Barron's. Enclose check or money order for total amount plus sales tax where applicable and 10% for postage and handling (minimum charge $3.75, Canada $4.00). Prices subject to change without notice.
ISBN PREFIX: 0-8120